Tan Tru

Larry Brooks

Library of Congress Control Number:
2014958095

Dedicated to all who served.

Tan Tru

Table of Contents

1 Introduction

2 The Powell's

3 Teenagers

4 Jordan High

5 High School Graduation and Beyond

6 Life in the Garage

7 Road Trip

8 Into the Army

9 Basic Training at Fort Ord

10 It's the Infantry

11 First Flight

12 Tigerland

13 Orders for Vietnam

14 Into Vietnam

14   The Ninth Infantry Division

15   Tan Tru

16   Combat Infantry Duty

17   Charlie Company

18   A Day in the Bowling Alley

19   Losing Hearts and Minds

20   Vicious Cycle

21   The Pink Palace

22   Hot Landing Zone

23   Machine Gun Time

24   A New Platoon Leader

25   April 17th

26   The Gunfighter Takes Over

27   Colonel Emerson and Bushmasters

28   The Plain of Reeds

29   Heartbreak and Shock

30   Body Escort Duty

31   Sad News on the Way Home

32   Riding on the Coast Starlight

33   Time Back in the U.S.A.

34   Bad News Back at Tan Tru

35   A Reluctant Warrior

36   Busted

37   Letters

38   Jitterbugging with Instant Staff Sergeants

39   September Sorrows

40   The Gunfighter Goes Down

41   Unnecessary Losses

42   Off the Line and Cannon Duty

43   A Christmas Truce and Hong Kong Revisited

44   Star Trek, Shock and Surprises

45   To the Freedom Bird

46   A Look Back

47   Home Again

48   A Return to Fort Ord

49   Stateside Duty

50 Witt

51 Hunter Liggett

52 Military Minimum Wage

53 Base Wanderings

54 An Official Reprimand

55 On Light Duty

56 Carmel by the Sea

57 Chewed Up and Spit Out

Postscript

Tan Tru

When I was growing up in the 1950's our Southern California neighborhood was a mix of frame houses, single-wide house trailers, chicken coops, small dairy operations, little manufacturing firms, a chrome plating company, a horse feed mill and a junk yard. My father purchased a parcel of land there when the town was still called Hynes in 1947, and he placed the box from the back of a junked moving van on the property for use as temporary shelter while he built a two bedroom frame house there with help from his brother-in-law Ed Larson.

My Uncle Ed had returned from infantry duty in World War II where he earned a couple of Purple Hearts in France. He was married to my dad's sister, Julia. Like so many other Midwesterners, Ed and Julia migrated to Southern California following the end of World War II.

We lived in Hynes, an unincorporated area that bordered the City of Long Beach on the north. Hynes and its adjacent unincorporated town of Clearwater later became the City of Paramount in 1957 when I was eight years old. Our house was located on the southwest corner of Jackson and Minnesota Streets and it eventually grew to be one of the largest in the neighborhood with five bedrooms, following two separate room addition projects over the period of a few years.

It was protected by a four foot high chain link fence built atop a three foot high retaining wall that paralleled our Jackson Street front sidewalk. Trash pick up service was still voluntary back then and our family disposed of refuse in a burn barrel next to a detached two-car garage at the west end of the property bounded by a culvert drained gravel driveway that dumped out on to Minnesota Street.

In those days our neighborhood was a white trash/redneck haven where little pre-teen waifs grew into teenage juvenile delinquents on the way to more felonious adult enterprises. Several young men who grew up living around our block would later become convicted murderers.

Across Jackson Street the Finley family lived in a three story Victorian whose clapboard exterior had been papered over on its sides with rock and oil roofing tile. It was the oldest house in the neighborhood pre-dating the little frame houses and trailers that populated the subdivided lands surrounding it. The house had a big front porch where Old Mrs. Finley would spend her days sitting and rocking in a chair as she watched over the neighborhood. Her aging husband rarely made an appearance.

Old man Finley had an identical twin brother married to the proprietor of a beauty shop across the alley and next door to our house across the street from the big Finley Victorian on Jackson Street. Arlene's Beauty Shop had a large glass window where we could see the old twin brother Finley watching television in his living room adjacent to the beauty shop room with its large hair drying machine chairs.

The old Finley next door, like his brother across the street, was in his eighties. He had a large magnifying glass attached to his TV screen that enabled him to see the black and white broadcasts.

He was a card carrying Communist, an avid reader of the People's Daily Worker newspaper. And even though he was visually impaired, he still had a driver's license. He drove a huge, immaculate 1956 Chrysler he meticulously parked in his garage facing the alley next to our kitchen by rolling back and forth a half dozen times, coming within inches of our chain link fence post with every pass, as he squared the big vehicle into position to enter his garage. As kids we would stand in our kitchen laughing and rooting him on as he worked to park the big Chrysler.

For a Communist he was a sweet old guy. In the summer he would invite my twin brother and me, and a couple of the other "poor" kids from the neighborhood along with him every week down to Cherry Beach in Long Beach. We would grab our towels and hop into his big back seat for the eight mile slow ride down Cherry Avenue to the beach. We kids would body surf and play in the water as old man Finley parked himself under an umbrella in the sand to read his Communist literature.

As we grew, three large older brothers and the prominent chain link fence protected our property and kept the neighborhood's human debris pretty much at bay, although from time to time when my twin brother and I would stray too far from the fortress we might be confronted by some of the neighborhood apes, and there were some rare occasions when we had to fend off a bully and run for it. But all in all it was pretty safe and a good place to grow up. Most of the neighbors were good people, and the bad guys left us alone. And it was home.

My father had earned a living working for bootleggers during the depths of America's Great Depression, a time when many others were selling apples on the streets to survive. Albartus James Brooks was born and raised in Hansboro, North Dakota, just two miles south of the Canadian border. He apparently knew the ropes when it came to moving goods in from Canada. Prohibition created new markets in the United States for Canadian whiskey. He helped nurture the enterprise.

His father, Sidney Brooks, died in 1918 when the Great Influenza swept across the United States when my father was only four years old. My grandmother, Margaret also bore Sidney a daughter, my Aunt Julia, in the year before Sidney's death. A few years after his death my grandmother married Charles Kessler in Hansboro, and they had a daughter, Rita, a few years later.

In the mid 1930's my father married Jeanne Kuperus. She was the third eldest of a dirt poor farm family with seven children from northern Minnesota. In her mid twenties at the time Mother was working as a housemaid in Minneapolis when she met and married my father, who by then was called Jim. Dad had been called Bartie by his mother, sisters and the rest of the folks in Hansboro while growing up. But he disliked the name so he had it changed to James Albartus Brooks when he reached legal age, and he thereafter became known as Jim.

Shortly following their marriage my parents had moved out west to the town of Scotia, in the redwoods on the North Coast of California, where Jeanne's older sister, Ann and her husband Eugene lived. My father found legitimate work there at the Pacific Lumber Mill where Eugene worked. It was a company town with company stores and my father was unhappy with lumber mill factory work and the damp North Coast weather. He'd developed a spirit of private entrepreneurship working as an independent contractor during the Depression and despite the company benefits, he never seemed able to get used to working for a company.

At the outbreak of World War II in December of 1941 my parents already had two baby children, my brother Dennis, born in 1940 and sister Marlene, born in the fall of 1941. With a wife and two babies, when the military draft came along, my dad was exempted.

Sometime around late 1942 or early 1943 the family left Scotia to find work in Southern California where another son, Dick, was born in 1943, followed by yet another son, Dwayne, born after the war in 1946.

Two more sons, Terry and I were born at Seaside Hospital in Long Beach, California in September of 1948. The folks had learned there were two of us only a few days before. My fraternal twin brother, weighing a paltry six pounds ten ounces, arrived six minutes after me.

2   The Powell's

When Terry and I were eleven years old, a skinny, brown haired kid by the name of Danny Powell and his family moved in next door. Danny was ten years old at the time. Their house was owned by my parents, purchased that year as a rental property. The lot had two houses, a tiny old frame house up front and newer three bedroom house on the back. The Powell's rented the three bedroom house.

At first Terry and I thought Danny was a bit of a twit but we still became close friends from the start anyway, not realizing at the time that for all practical purposes we had just inherited another brother. Danny had two younger sisters, Becky, age eight; and Sharon, who was about four. Terry and I became the brothers Danny lacked as we kind of informally adopted him as younger little brother by default.

He was kind of a goofball in our eyes perhaps due to the fact that he had never lived with the pressures of having older brothers around to judge his actions and correct his dorky behavior. Terry and I took it upon ourselves to bring him up to speed as to what we considered to be hip as best we could through the years that he lived next door, years he spent more time in our home than his own including mealtimes.

We did the normal things kids do. We played baseball and pick up football games and hung out down the street at the Wesley Gaines Elementary School which had a huge grass field, ball diamonds, a basketball court, and tetherball poles.

We enjoyed movies. There were two movie theaters in the nearby Bixby Knolls district of nearby Long Beach where we escaped to take in movies on a regular basis, The Towne and The Crest. On most Sunday afternoons the folks would dump the three of us at one of these venues where we would watch double features. After the movies our fertile young minds would often transport us into the characters we watched on the big screen.

After watching "The Magnificent Seven" for the twelfth or thirteenth time I became the leader Chris, the Yul Brenner character, Terry would alternate between Steve McQueen and the James Colburn guy with the switchblade. Danny always had a personal flair for the melodramatic, so he would be "the Kid", the Horst Buckholtz character who wanted to be a tough gunman but was really just another poor Mexican dirt farmer. We killed off endless childhood hours in our two family yards in Paramount fighting make believe banditos in defense of poor Mexicans and their little dirt farmer village.

3   Teenagers

As we grew into our early teenage years our lives were increasingly intruded upon by our parents. By the age of fourteen Terry and I were called upon to work after school and on Saturdays on small construction projects with our father, who became a small residential building contractor. He had started out owning an aluminum awning business then he branched out into residential remodeling and room additions.

My mother and father were Depression Era Dutch and Irish stock, respectively. When the Billy Graham Crusade came to the Los Angeles Coliseum in September of 1963 they both became more serious about their religion, especially my father. He had been raised a Roman Catholic, but as an adult he became an evangelical Protestant. When the Billy Graham crusade came to Los Angeles he served as a volunteer counselor throughout the event.

This greatly pleased our mother who was raised in the Dutch Reformed Church, Protestant people who seriously frowned on drinking, carousing, womanizing, and sin in general.

On the other hand Danny Powell's parents were nominal Southern Baptists who seemed to be a bit more tolerant of sin… in the country music sense. Larry and Ruth Powell were most certainly country folk, coming to Paramount from Arkansas by way of Fresno, California.

Larry Powell was without question the laziest man I had ever known, never having held a job for more than a week. He was a fairly handsome man in his thirties who loved to shop for new cars and he considered himself some kind of a mechanic. But he could never seem to find work because, as he would tell you, "I sold my tools and I "caint" make change". So he passed his days lying around his house smoking cigarettes and watching TV... between naps. He died of a heart attack before he reached forty.

Ruth was more industrious. I suppose she was considered pretty attractive in those days. We calculated she had to have been only 15 or 16 years old when Danny was born so she was only around 26 or 27 when the Powell's moved next door. My mother helped find her work to support their family (and to keep up with the rent) at the Douglas Aircraft plant in Long Beach where my mother had worked for several years. Rumor had it Ruth flirted around a bit down at the aircraft plant...in the country music sense.

My father was entering his early fifties then. He was a barrel-chested five foot-eight with forearms like Popeye the Sailor. He had a natural, quiet demeanor and spent most evening hours working out in the garage, tinkering on various would be invention projects, keeping peacefully away from my mother and the clamor that filled our busy house. Since he was an independent general contractor who specialized in home remodels, he joined the local Christian Businessmen's organization to help network his business, and the folks became regular members of the North Long Beach Brethren Church when Terry and I were about fourteen years old.

As we reached high school age the folks decided it was time to sell the house and rental properties in Paramount. As a consequence the Powell's decided to move out to a rental house in the City of Artesia, a few miles east, while my parents looked to buy a house a few miles away in North Long Beach. We didn't know it until later that much of the motivation for that move was to save Terry and me from the clutches of Satan.

It was after our sophomore year at Paramount High School when the folks made the move to the small 1950's tract house in North Long Beach. It would be a new experience for Terry and me, living in a normal residential neighborhood.

Even though the new residence was only two miles from our old house in Paramount, it was in a different school district; Long Beach Unified, which meant Terry and I would have to uproot from our friends and teachers, and transfer to a different high school in Long Beach.

We were unhappy. We both played football at Paramount High, following in the tradition of all our three older brothers who played football on the varsity team at Paramount High. Now we had to leave our friends and our family tradition there.

Since Terry and I had attended the same district schools from kindergarten all the way through tenth grade, the Paramount Superintendent of Schools personally called our parents and invited them to allow us to continue to attend Paramount High School through an inter-district transfer. But it was of no use. The folks had a plan, and over our strong objections the folks said no.

Our three older brothers had pretty much sealed our fate. The oldest, Dennis, had traumatized mother by declaring his atheism following his freshman year at Long Beach State College. Brother Dick, serving in the army in Vietnam by then, had taken to smoking cigarettes and drinking beer, clearly mortal sins by my mother's measure, and Dwayne had just completed a storied career at Paramount High School by arriving home at five in the morning several times reeking of cheap vodka.

Surprisingly for all of this ungodly Brooks brothers behavior they all graduated high school with clean rap sheets and went on to college for a year or two before dropping out and heading into military service, and marriage.

Still, the folks were insistent upon salvaging the youngest boys of the brood from the influences of the evil Paramount High School crowd. The North Long Beach Brethren Church elders had apparently convinced the folks that our continued attendance of Paramount High School was a gateway to a life of sin and debauchery, and nearby Jordan High, well attended by other North Long Beach Brethren youth, would surely save us from the clutches of Satan.

4   Jordan High

Terry and I unhappily entered the eleventh grade at David Starr Jordan High School in Long Beach in September of 1964. By this time we were the last of the Brooks children living at home. Dennis was now married, having just completed a three year army hitch the year before, Sister Marlene was off and away married, Brother Dick was now in the Army in Vietnam, and Dwayne was living out of the house with a buddy and attending Compton Junior College.

To add insult to injury, in addition to our exile to Jordan High, Terry and I were ordered to attend Sunday school and church services every Sunday and attend Wednesday night Bible studies at the now nearby North Long Beach Brethren Church.

We hated all of it, and the only thing that kept us both from going nuts was having each other to commiserate with while looking forward to high school graduation in two years, when we might free ourselves from the clutches of the North Long Beach Brethren Church, Jordan High School, and the constant string of guilt trips that were lain upon us by our increasingly pious, nut case mother.

Shortly after the move to Long Beach and no doubt sensing our mother's descent into hysterical victim hood, the old man decided to build an addition to the garage behind our house for Terry and me to occupy. Our mother had lived through the Great Depression growing up dirt poor and hungry in Minnesota.

She had borne six children within a span of eight years, and worked ten years at the Douglas Aircraft factory. So at the ripe old age of fifty she decided it was time to begin to live her life as a full time Christian martyr. And that she did. In fact she was to make an art of her martyrdom which was to last throughout the rest of her life, for another thirty-seven years.

In 1965 our dad completed a "shop" addition to the unattached garage behind the house in North Long Beach, pirating in two small bedrooms plus a bath and shower that he hid from the building inspectors. Terry and I cheerfully moved out there at the beginning of our senior year of high school. It would prove to provide suitable transitional housing for us with the added benefit that we could arrive home nights undetected and free of breath inspections, and mother's hysterics.

5   Graduation and Beyond

Terry and I played on the varsity football team at Jordan High in our senior year. We were both starters on the defensive line, and the experience helped us to partially assimilate into the Jordan High School culture. In truth we made some friends, although we both always felt alienated there. Our social lives didn't amount to much and by the second semester of our senior year we had both accumulated sufficient graduation credits, which permitted us to attend classes for only morning elective sessions, and were out of school every day at noon. The schedule allowed us to take afternoon part time jobs at the R.D. Mathis Company, a small microelectronics company in Long Beach. We made the minimum wage there and it provided us with gas and fooling around money.

By this time we had mastered the art of evading Sunday morning church services. We would drive our own shared automobile to the church, fake coughing spells and quietly slip out the back of the congregation at the start of services. It was not difficult in a church that had regular attendance of 700 or more for its Sunday services.

Following high school graduation Terry and I exercised independent identities. It was bad enough having names that rhymed, but as small children our mother had paraded us around as her personal accessories. We were even dressed alike until we took it upon ourselves to dress differently at age seven.

Three months after high school graduation we dutifully registered with the Selective Service System when we turned eighteen in September of 1966. The Vietnam War was raging then and we were told we could expect to be drafted within six to nine months unless we were enrolled in college full time and obtained college deferments.

By this time brother Dick, who dropped out of Long Beach State College following his freshman year, was back in town after three years in the army and Dwayne, having volunteered for the draft the year before, had taken his turn serving in the Army in Germany. Dick and Dennis had both enlisted and served in the United States Army Security Agency (ASA) and both of them had done tours in Vietnam.

Our finances dictated we attend a junior college. Since our parents offered no college funds for us we had to pay our own ways to school. Junior college was cheap and our jobs at the R.D. Mathis Company earned us enough to pay for school, provided we continued living out in the folk's garage.

Our house was in the Long Beach City College (LBCC) district and Terry decided to attend there. To be different I opted to attend Compton Junior College (CJC) using a friend's address in Paramount, which was in the Compton College district. Terry and I began our freshman college years attending different schools for the first time in our young lives as Danny Powell began his senior year at Richard Gahr High School in Artesia, California where he played trumpet in the school band.

6 Life in the Garage

In June of 1967 Terry and I finished our freshman years of junior college and Danny Powell graduated high school. Over the course of that first year the three of us kept in close contact with each other. Also by this time Terry had managed to perfect the art of managing our mother's hysterics. He embraced the "Eddie Haskell" approach, named in honor of Wally Cleaver's TV show pal on "Leave it to Beaver". Terry simply told mother whatever was convenient to get her off of his back regardless of its veracity or lack thereof, an art that would years later serve him well in a law career.

Conversely, I found myself becoming more and more disgusted with our mother's intrusions, preaching and harassment. Looking back at that time it seems her unstated intent was to simply drive us out of the garage without having to literally order us to fly the coop.

Terry seemed to sense this and hatched his own personal strategy to stay in the garage rent free while attending school and maintaining his draft deferment. He figured it was really a pretty sweet deal, and in retrospect I suppose he was right. By refusing to take the old lady seriously he was able to ignore her rants and self pitying with a clear conscious while he concentrated on his own future.

At the same time I made the mistake of taking the old broad way too seriously, and so increasingly my reaction to her was anger. I could envision but one solution, to leave home, knowing that leaving the garage also meant going to work full time, and going to work which would render me unable to continue to carry a full time academic load. I would lose my 2-S draft deferment. The dilemma was compounded by the fact that the Vietnam War was getting nastier with every passing month.

In late June I visited the dingy offices of the draft board in Long Beach to inquire as to my fate should I enroll in less than a full academic load come fall. I was advised that in such case I would be reclassified 1-A by September and I could expect to be drafted around January or February of 1968.

For the next week I mulled over my options. Should I remain in the garage, attending college and put up with my mother, or face possible injury or death in the jungles of Vietnam?

A couple weeks later I made the fateful decision to risk facing the Viet Cong rather than putting up with my mother for another three years. I decided, in a fit of youthful insanity, to get the whole thing over with and volunteer for the draft. This pushed the entire schedule ahead by five or six months. For some reason it never even occurred to me to consider joining the service in return for a guaranteed military occupation that might not get me killed.

A couple days later Danny Powell, fresh out of high school, made a secret visit to the Selective Service office and arranged to be drafted on the same day as me. When he proudly announced this I was furious. But the deed was done and there was nothing anyone could do about it.

7   Road Trip

That summer Danny Powell and I were both killing time until August before we went into the service so we took a road trip together. We took my 1961 Ford Falcon east to Fort Smith, Arkansas where Danny wanted to visit a grandmother. We drove Old Route 66 through Arizona, New Mexico and Texas, camping in the car in parks and wide spaces along the road.

On our fourth of fifth afternoon on the road we pulled into a greasy spoon gravel parking lot in the town of Erick in the Oklahoma panhandle. It was on a Sunday. Pulling to a stop I had to pump the brakes to get brake pressure and knew something was amiss with the Falcon. We had a blown wheel bearing on the right rear axle. As it was Sunday there was no place to get a new bearing so we were stuck for the night in the gravel parking lot in front of the greasy spoon right there on Route 66 in Erick.

The local police chief was making his rounds and stopped to inquire. We told him our problem and asked him where a motel might be found. It turned out that in July of 1967 Erick, Oklahoma had no motel, or hotel for that matter. So the chief offered to let Danny and me sleep in the town jail.

We had both had visions of Mayberry. So at that point and so we accepted the offer. So the chief said he would return around 9 PM and ride us on over. When we got to the jail that night we found the facilities to be quite a bit more Spartan than we imagined. It was a long, red brick room on the back of the small police station of no more than six feet in width, with one two foot by two foot barred window. It contained three steel bunk beds with two inch bare mattresses situated end to end with a toilet and small wash basin at the back end opposite the jail door, which the chief locked behind him as he was leaving.

It was 103 degrees in Erick that night and the jail had virtually no air circulation. Try as we might neither Danny nor I could sleep a wink. Our salvation finally arrived about 3AM when the chief brought in a young drunk. We told him we were ready to leave and he accommodated us. We went back to the Falcon and Danny went to sleep on the front seat while I slept outside sprawled up on the roof.

On Monday morning the Erick Ford dealer opened around eight. I jacked up the Falcon and pulled off the axle with the burnt bearing and brought it in there. The service department sold me a new bearing and installed it on the axle for me right there. They charged me just $10.35. I took the axle and bearing back to the greasy spoon and installed it back on the Falcon, lugged up the wheel and we headed out that morning in the direction of Fort Smith. We later learned that Erick, Oklahoma was the home town of Roger Miller. The whole episode gave new meaning to the song "Chug-a-lug Chug-a-lug".

After visiting Danny's Grandmother in Fort Smith and playing a round of golf at the Fort Smith Country Club in 105 degree heat we headed north for North Dakota where we visited my 83 year old Grandmother. She was in a nursing home in Rolla. After a day there we headed back toward California, making it to Billings, Montana the first night. The next morning we took off and drove straight through to Lovelock Nevada, a stretch of more than 1100 miles. Two days later we were back home in Long Beach.

8 Into the Army

On August 23, 1967 our post cards in hand with greetings from the President of the United States of America, Danny Powell and I met the bus in front of the federal building on Ocean Boulevard in downtown Long Beach at 8:00 AM as directed. Accompanied by somewhere on the order of forty other military inductees to be, we were bound for the military induction station in downtown Los Angeles, where we would join a couple hundred additional young men from throughout Los Angeles County.

After a morning and afternoon of physical inspections and other tests the group was lined up and was sworn into the United States Army, and herded on to busses headed to Fort Ord near Monterey, California.

Standing on the sidewalk outside the induction station in stunned silence I watched the busses drive away without me. I had failed to pass my physical examination, compliments of a twelve inch surgical scar on my left side, a remnant of kidney surgery at the age of nine. The doctor at the induction station told me they would check with the urologist who had operated on me nine years earlier and then make a determination as to my physical fitness for military service. I was to be called back two months later.

Of course, given the mass of humanity passing through the LA induction center, I would later conclude that the odds of actually being ordered back two months later were practically zero. I did not understand that I had, for all practical intents, been relieved of my military obligation. The Selective Service system would doubtfully have the time or resources to track down my urologist to pry into my medical history. I didn't realize it, but I was free to begin my life without a military obligation.

Be that as it may, there was a hitch. Danny Powell was on one of the busses. And rightly or wrongly I felt like I was a big part of the reason he was bound for Fort Ord.

So that afternoon I found myself standing in front of Corky's restaurant around the corner from the Los Angeles Induction Station feeling both relief and guilt as I headed for a telephone booth to call my brother Dwayne for a ride back to Long Beach.

When I arrived back at home mother was unhappy. It was a setback. Five down and one to go once again became four down and two to go. Although her disappointment with my return to the fold was plainly evident she need not have worried. I would not be there long. Danny Powell was on the bus to Fort Ord without me and I was about to embark on a foolish mission of saving Private Powell.

The following day I visited my urologist's office in Long Beach on my own. I hadn't seen Dr. Larry Avocado for many years but, except for the gray hair, he looked the same. I explained my situation and he proudly had his office assistant type out a letter for me on the spot. It was a clean 100% cured clearance to get drafted.

My concern now was to catch up with Danny Powell. The following day, on August 25th Dwayne took me back to the Los Angeles Induction Station. That evening I too was on a bus headed for Fort Ord.

9   Basic Training at Fort Ord

I arrived at the Fort Ord Reception Station that night where the army welcomed us to military service by jerk ass corporals screaming at us as our bus pulled to a stop in the darkness of night.   It was a grouping of barracks for temporary billeting and it was also the place where the barbers cut your hair in about sixty seconds, and where boots, socks, underwear, fatigues, dog tags and ball caps were issued.

It wasn't until the next morning that I saw Danny standing in a disheveled formation with another group of new soldiers with whom I was not permitted to speak. In 1967 a meningitis outbreak had infected Fort Ord, and to prevent the disease from spreading, newly minted GI's were separated by platoons of 50 trainees each from the minute they arrived. Each platoon of men was forbidden to mingle close enough to infect others.

Danny and I were assigned to separate platoons in the same basic training company. We spent a day at the Reception Station where we had our heads shaved into buzz cuts, issued olive drab green fatigue uniforms with our names stitched to our chests with white tags above our names that identified us as meningitis isolated basic training trainees.

We were assigned to Bravo Company, 3rd Battalion, and 1st Training Brigade (B-3-1) for basic combat training. As best as I can recall I was in the second platoon while Danny was in the fourth. About half of my platoon was made up of Hawaiians and guys from Guam. The other half, as well as the other three platoons in the company, were all kids from southern California, ninety percent of who were white.

There are two basic U.S. Army categories, Regular Army, whose serial numbers began with "RA", and draftees whose serial numbers began with "US". Being an "RA" or a "US" pretty much defined a soldier. "RA's" had enlisted for a minimum three year hitch with a guaranteed military occupational specialty (MOS). A draftee was a "US" who had to serve only two years who's MOS would be assigned by the army. Of the 200 trainees in B-3-1 ninety percent were "US's", like Danny and like me.

Basic training lasted eight weeks. It sucked and we were constantly berated. In those days the army's philosophy was to break us down mentally before molding us into highly trained killing machines.

The Fort Ord meningitis restrictions confined us exclusively to our own fifty man platoons with no opportunity to mingle with members of other platoons in the company. We would see members of other platoons at training sites and in the chow hall but were forbidden from even speaking to members of other platoons. It also meant we were confined to base for all eight weeks with no off base passes and no outside visitors.

On the Sunday after our fourth week of training the company was allowed some free time to rest on the lawn on the sunny side of our barracks. All four platoons sat resting outside smoking cigarettes, separated by platoon.

Danny Powell was in the group next to ours and I sneaked over and for the first time since we had been inducted into the Army we had a chance to talk. We had about fifteen minutes before a drill instructor busted up our conversation. But while there Danny introduced me to a member of his platoon he had befriended. Like Danny, George Vander Dussen was from Artesia. He was a couple years older than me and was a dairy farmer with a young pretty wife.

The meningitis restrictions at Fort Ord required that the barracks windows remained open twenty-four hours a day. When we were rousted awake each pre dawn morning the interior of the barracks would be fog bound from Pacific Ocean moisture inside until the heaters came on and cleared it out.

Basic training taught us a lot. We learned about the Army and its structure. We learned how to shoot a rifle and throw a grenade, how to march, how to wear a uniform and we learned the meaning of "service". It's something you cannot really understand until you lose your personal freedom and become the property of your country.

We learned the world was a big place and there were forces in the world that subjected young men to hostility that came not just from enemies far away but from people who could lord over you, shout at you, emaciate you, and in the name of training you for hardships and peril, could subjugate a human being in the name of the American government.

10   It's The Infantry

The culmination of basic training was graduation. At graduation we were promoted from Private Grade E-1 to Private E-2 and our pay was increased from around $65 to $75 a month. Aside from the graduation ceremonies, where family and relatives could come to attend, the most important thing about graduation was learning much of your fate.

After marching around the parade field at the graduation ceremony, the trainees returned to barracks where duty orders were posted. If you were a draftee you had just spent eight weeks wondering what the Army was going to do with you. Along the way you have taken a number of aptitude tests to help the Army determine how best to utilize your talents.

My brother Dwayne, like me, had been a draftee two years earlier. Following his basic training he was ordered to attend nuclear weapons maintenance training in Albuquerque, New Mexico before assignment to Germany. That sounded pretty good to me.

When I finally made my way up to the board to read my orders, I learned that of the nearly two hundred draftees in B-3-1 about six had been assigned to truck driving school. All of the other draftees, including Danny and me, were assigned an 11B10 infantry MOS, and almost all of those ordered into the infantry, Danny among them, were to remain at Fort Ord for eight more weeks of advanced infantry training (AIT). For some reason I was one of only a half a dozen trainees from the company ordered to ship out to Fort Polk, Louisiana for AIT.

The infantry training facility at Fort Polk was called Tigerland. It was dedicated solely for training infantrymen for combat service in Vietnam. One hundred percent of Tigerland AIT graduates were assigned directly to infantry units in Vietnam following the completion of their training.

The decision to order more than nearly every conscript completing basic training at Fort Ord in the fall of 1967 into infantry service was based on only one single criterion. It was based on the numbers of fresh bodies the United States of America needed to toss into the meat grinder that was infantry service in Vietnam.

So on the last day of my basic training I finally knew where I was headed and what I would be doing and there was nothing I could do to change it. I was in the vortex with all the others. It would send me into the paddies and jungles of Southeast Asia with a rifle. I knew I needed to learn how to survive with my brothers who had been cast into the same ugly vortex.

11 A First Flight

I had never flown in an airplane in my life. A bus transported about twenty-five of us that very afternoon from Fort Ord Basic Training graduation to the Oakland Airport. Most of those I was traveling with were bound for Fort Sam Houston in San Antonio, Texas to be trained as medics. After five or six months training most would be assigned to infantry units as field medics throughout Vietnam. They were the same as infantry grunts, only assigned to go to the most dangerous spot in every firefight. To try to save the life of a casualty. After dropping them off at San Antonio six of us were to stay on the plane to continue on to Louisiana.

Five minutes after our lift off from the Oakland Airport the pilot came up on the PA system and told us we had a red light indicating the forward gear (the front wheels) had failed to fully retract. He calmly informed us that we would fly out over the Pacific and dump our fuel, and then return to Oakland.

We returned to Oakland after about 30 minutes and landed. As we did, fire trucks and other emergency vehicles, including ambulances, rolled along side next to our runway as we touched down.

We taxied to the terminal and the plane load of young soldiers exited. We all headed for the airport terminal bar. Most of us were under the legal drinking age of 21 but wearing uniforms no one checked IDs. Somewhat unnerved by the flight experience we sat there and drank for two hours while the plane was checked out.

Two dozen guys who had just spent eight weeks in isolated, meningitis restricted basic training at Fort Ord sitting at a little commuter bar at the Oakland Airport, having just departed an airplane that had just made an emergency return to Oakland after dumping its fuel, were sitting at the bar. We drank. It turned out the red indicator light was screwed up and the forward gear was just fine.

12   Tigerland

After the stop at Fort Sam Houston in San Antonio, Texas where we dropped off the Medical Corps trainees, we took off for England Air Force Base in Alexandria, Louisiana. From there we were bussed through the pines to Fort Polk's Tigerland. We were quickly assigned to barracks in North Fort Polk, Louisiana. I was assigned to Training Company D/4/3.

I found my bunk and crashed. One minute later I was roused by a fellow trainee bequeathed with a temporary sergeant striped armband who told me I was not allowed to sleep. Most of the other trainees there had already been there for two or three days and the cadre had assigned leadership arm bands to a few of them.

At this point I had not slept for more than fifty hours. It was a warm Sunday afternoon. Fort Polk was a sugar pined mountain place. I decided that sleep was necessary come hell or high water so I ducked outside and walked about 300 yards out into the forest behind the wooden barracks where I gathered some pine straw over a flat area and lied down. I must have slept there undisturbed under the pines for five hours. When I woke up and made my way back to the barrack at dusk where it was finally okay to sleep and my absence had gone unnoticed. The next morning we started nine weeks of advanced infantry training at Tigerland: Training Place of Infantrymen Bound for Vietnam.

I thought about Danny Powell at AIT back at Fort Ord. I was glad knowing he was there with George Vander Dussen who became Danny's best buddy.

I had held out some hope that in AIT we would be treated a little better than we were at basic training, at least in terms of non-stop personal humiliation of trainees. I was wrong. At Fort Polk the training was physically and mentally harsher than basic. We were allowed to sleep only three and one-half to five hours a night and the training was intense, physically demanding and difficult, made only worse by the specter of a one year tour of infantry duty in Vietnam hanging out there in front of us.

We were humiliated throughout training at Tigerland. It was basic combat training on steroids. Day after day we were herded on to cattle trucks and driven out to training sites in the pine covered hills of Louisiana. We were screamed at by the cadre as we labored to learn how to operate every small arm the army had.

We were dehumanized and hardened. We slept in the rain and ran in full gear through weeks of training and told we would likely die in the jungles of Vietnam because we let our guard down or we were too stupid to survive. We were dogs herded from one kennel of training to the next.

We were also underfed. If you found yourself in the last 20% in the chow line at breakfast you settled for toast, cereal or a banana. The eggs, bacon, hotcakes, and sausage were long gone. The same was true for the mainstays at lunch and dinner. This situation lasted for the first six weeks of training when the food shortage situation suddenly ended.

It turned out that some of our asshole superiors in D/4/3 at Tigerland had been selling our food off base for a few extra bucks. They had apparently been busted, but no announcements were made. Adequate food rations just magically appeared at the start of week seven.

The only positive of having trained at Tigerland was nearly all the NCO cadre and trainers there were Vietnam infantry veterans. So we got the straight scoop. Our days there started with pre-dawn formation and roll call. After chow we formed up again and were then herded on to the open, benched, wooden railed trailers. We would be hauled out to each training area for the day's training. It got colder by the day in Louisiana as November waned into December and we froze our asses in those open trailers.

We were given two weeks leave for Christmas, 1967 and I was able to fly home the holidays. It was a real treat to get warm for awhile. At the same time Danny Powell was given leave having already completed AIT at Fort Ord. We compared notes about training. Danny and George's AIT at Fort Ord was just an eight week cycle. Mine at Tigerland was nine weeks and so I had to return to Fort Polk to complete it following the Christmas/New Year's holidays. After ten more days at Tigerland I would get my orders for Vietnam. When ordered to Vietnam you were given a 30 day leave before you shipped out. This meant I would be back at home for another leave in Long Beach just two weeks later.

Meanwhile, Danny Powell's entire training company had been assigned to report to Fort Hood, Texas, so he was headed out there right after New Year's. They were told that at Fort Hood they would be assembled into a new battalion and deployed to Vietnam together as a new unit a couple of months later. This was quite different from what I would be doing. I would be sent to a replacement battalion in Vietnam and from there I would be assigned as a replacement to a unit already deployed there. This meant that I would not see Danny again until we both (hopefully) returned from our tours in Vietnam.

At the Christmas holiday Danny and I were both granted ten days leave, so I headed back to Long Beach from Louisiana and Danny along with George Vander Dussen came down from Fort Ord.

On New Year's Eve Terry, Danny and I found our way over to George Vander Dussen's house in Artesia. George's wife greeted us all there and shortly thereafter she left for dinner with George's twin sister, leaving the four of us to spend the evening there downing several six packs of beer, and discussing the status of the world at the beginning of 1968. Danny, George and I were headed for Vietnam and

Terry surprised us all with the news that he had joined the Long Beach City College football team, playing backup defensive back. It was a great drunken night to remember.

13 Orders for Vietnam

Two days later I caught a morning flight back to Louisiana to complete my infantry training. The culmination of training at Tigerland was what seemed like a fifty mile march out for a week long bivouac. The fact that it was 20 degrees and *raining* did not matter. It was a week of cold misery sleeping in pup tents on ice in Louisiana's freezing rain. A few of the guys came down with pneumonia and were hospitalized. Having failed to complete the training cycle meant they would be recycled and given the opportunity to do it all again.

On our final day of training we were herded into a chapel where the battalion chaplain addressed the assembled men of D/4/3 and other training companies in our cycle. He talked about the dangers of combat somberly telling us there was a probability that about 5% of us would not survive our Vietnam tours.

When our training was finally over they held a parade and graduation ceremony for us. On a sunny, early January afternoon we stood on a soggy wet parade field, in a huge formation with hundreds of Tigerland graduates, and listened as Senator Russell Long, Democrat of the Great State of Louisiana, graced us with stories of his naval service in World War II.

Later that day I was given my orders to report to the Oakland Army Base in thirty days on 9 February 1968 for transfer to the 90th Replacement Battalion, Republic of Vietnam (RVN). Rick Bryant, a Long Beach buddy of mine in D/4/3, and I caught a bus to Love Field in Dallas where we caught standby tickets to LA for our thirty day leaves.

Looking back at that time back in the garage in Long Beach, counting down the days is pretty much a blur. But I remember Terry and I got a letter from Danny Powell from Fort Hood. It looked like he and his unit would hit Vietnam some time in late March, about a month or two after I would arrive there. They were forming a new unit, the 198th Light Infantry Brigade which would become part of the Americal Division (23rd Infantry Division). I, on the other hand, would be sent as an individual replacement to any one of several divisions or regiments in Vietnam. I would not know where I would be assigned in Vietnam until I got there.

In his letter, Danny said he would not live through Vietnam. Although Danny always had a flair for dramatic it was clear that he was serious. None of us bound for infantry duty at the height of the Vietnam War had any illusions about the dangers we faced. But I had never allowed myself to believe that I would not survive. Terry and I were both disturbed by Danny's letter and the fact that I would not be able to see him again until we both completed our tours of duty in Vietnam which bothered us a lot.

Home in Long Beach on leave, about two weeks before I was due to report to Oakland, Danny Powell just walked up to our house one morning. Amid smiles and greetings he told us he had decided to take a visit to home to see me before I headed across the pond. He had simply gone A.W.O.L. Laughing he said, "What can they do to me? Send me to Vietnam?"

He spent a great week with us before placing a call to Fort MacArthur in Los Angeles to turn himself into the military authorities. The Military Police showed up the next day and shipped him back to Texas.

I later learned that when he arrived back at his unit at Fort Hood his company commander called him out and stood him in front of his company formation and lectured his troops. Standing him at attention in front of his company he told them what Private Daniel Powell had done, violating military regulations by going absent without leave, a serious criminal offense, just to visit his best friend in California who was on leave before heading to Vietnam…and that Private Powell had more "guts" than anyone else in the company for doing what he had done. That was the full extent of Private Daniel Lee Powell's "punishment" when he got back to Fort Hood.

A few days before reporting to Oakland my folks drove me up to San Rafael where my Uncle Bill and Aunt Dorothy lived. They had a house nestled high in the redwoods in the Dominican Hill section on a lot with a spectacular view of both San Francisco and San Pablo Bays. Bill was one of my mother's younger brothers. She had five brothers in all and one older sister. Following World War II Bill and Dorothy had settled there. Bill worked in a local lumber yard and Dorothy worked in the meat department of a Safeway store in San Rafael.

Mother's brothers were nothing like her. Like his brothers, Uncle Bill enjoyed his life. He was known to imbibe, he was easygoing, and he was not one to be found in a church on Sunday morning. He was one of my favorite uncles and his wife, Dorothy was nothing short of a sweet angel. They were gracious hosts who genuinely enjoyed spoiling guests in their beautiful home, a home Bill built from the ground up over a period of many years. We spent a final night there before heading to Oakland.

14   Into Vietnam

The Oakland Army Base was a warehouse with bunk beds. Oakland was the place where U.S. Army soldiers headed for Vietnam mixed with the soldiers returning. It took about two days of processing before the Vietnam bound boarded buses for Travis Air Force Base near the City of Fairfield, some thirty or so miles east of Oakland. Chartered civilian airplanes at Travis were used to take soldiers back from Vietnam via Travis as well as ferry us over.

It was at Oakland where we learned that something they were calling the Tet Offensive was occurring in Vietnam. There were television sets hanging from walls spaced around the bunks there covering the news events in Vietnam. Many of the returnees arriving at Oakland for processing just looked at us and shook their heads. It was apparent that bad stuff was happening.

On the long flight to Vietnam from Travis AFB we made a refueling stop in Okinawa, Japan then headed for Bien Hoa Air Force Base located a bit northwest of Saigon. Our descent in corkscrew mode over Bien Hoa to avoid possible enemy fire was interrupted at around 10,000 feet as the pilot called over the speaker to announce our flight was being diverted to Tan Son Nhut International, the civilian airport in Saigon, in order to avoid ground artillery fire occurring around Bien Hoa.

Arriving in Vietnam the heat and humidity mixed with the smells of diesel and smoke assaulted our senses and marked the beginning of what portended to be 365 days of non-stop perspiration. We landed at Tan Son Nhut International Airport, now deserted except for us and patrolling infantry troops of the 196th Light Infantry Brigade.

The hard ground fighting in Saigon that had drawn in units from jungles and rice fields all around Saigon had mostly ended just hours before our touch down but we heard there was still heavy fighting going on up north at a town called Hue. The U.S. infantry troops patrolling the Ton Son Nhut Airport looked weary and caked in red dust. Watching them I was struck by the thought that most of them were just like me just a few months before. And now they were battle hardened combat veterans.

The airport terminal was an open air facility with a high overhead shelter and with a couple dozen twelve to twenty foot wide wooden booths that housed civilian airline reps and ticketing agents for the likes of Pan Am and TWA, all now   vacant except for us and the patrolling U.S. troopers.

Shortly after our arrival four or five military busses arrived to transport us to the 90th Replacement Battalion which was located on the road from Saigon between the village of Bien Hoa and the huge army logistics base at Long Bien. We were escorted through a still smoldering Saigon by army gun jeeps fore and aft of our bus caravan and two Huey helicopter gun ships overhead. Looking out through heavy gauge wire screened bus windows much of Saigon looked like a bullet scarred, pockmarked, smoking, smoldering mess.

The stay at the 90th Replacement was brief. After a few short hours we were assembled into a formation of more than 400 new arrivals in a large open field. Standing on a raised platform before us a sergeant held a megaphone. There were assignment points behind him with signs reading 1st Infantry Division, 4th Infantry Division, 9th Infantry Division, 25th Infantry Division, 101st Airborne Division, and the rest of the units in country. When your name was called you were to report to the unit.

As he was calling out the names there was a lone soldier sitting on a bench to the right of the large formation, under a wooden canopy playing a "bro-box" blurting out "Light My Fire" by the Doors so loud that it made it hard to hear the sergeant up front. Yet he was ignored. Twenty-three minutes of "Light My Fire" went uninterrupted as the sergeant called out our unit assignments. When he was calling out names for the 9th Infantry Division I finally heard my name. So I finally knew where I was headed.

15 The Ninth Infantry Division

The units of the Ninth Infantry Division had arrived in Vietnam in December of 1966 through January of 1967. Its original division base camp in Vietnam was a place called Bearcat, located a few miles northwest of Saigon. But the division was sent to Vietnam for one main reason. It was to assault the huge enemy Viet Cong stronghold of the Mekong Delta, a huge, flat swampland of winding rivers, rice paddies and jungles in the southern part of South Vietnam that was home to about 80% of the country's population. The Delta was the "rice bowl" for the country, and it was the last part of the country where large scale American forces were to be sent.

In early 1968 the Ninth Division was completing construction of its new base camp at Dong Tam, located a few miles to the west of the City of My Tho, about 40 miles southwest of Saigon. The division was made up of three brigades. At Dong Tam the Second Brigade of the Ninth Division made up the division's Mobile Riverine Force (MRF). It teamed with the U.S. Navy to conduct combat operations from large river floating troop ships from which infantry troops undertook river shore assaults from Navy landing craft.

The Division's First and Third Brigades consisted of mechanized armor battalions, units that conducted operations from mechanized troop carriers, and regular infantry battalions.

As best I can recall there were about 50 or 60 men assigned to the Ninth Division from the 90th Replacement on the day I went through. We were placed on deuce and a half army trucks and driven to Bearcat. At Bearcat we were issued M-16 rifles and steel pot helmets and liners to complete our jungle fatigue clothing that had been issued us at the 90th Replacement. It was there our group was parceled out to individual battalions. I was one of four men assigned to report to the 2nd battalion, 60th Infantry located at a place called Tan Tru.

We caught a re-supply deuce and a half ton truck to Tan An, a town with an airfield and an artillery fire base. It was located along a paved highway that was the last stop before hitting the road to Tan Tru, a twelve kilometer ride over a dirt roadway. At Tan An, the four of us hitched a ride on a jeep headed for Tan Tru. On the jeep was a 1st Lieutenant by the name of Lieutenant Sargent and his driver.

As we headed for Tan Tru Lieutenant Sargent looked back at us and asked if we had ammunition for our newly minted M-16's. We said no. So he handed us four magazines of ammunition apiece and we each locked and loaded our rifles for the first time in Vietnam.

On that day on Tan Tru Road I met Bill Sommers, Ronald Cavett, and another fellow whose name I cannot recall because when we arrived at Tan Tru that guy was plucked away. He was some kid from Chicago and he was picked at random to become the battalion commander's aid.

At Tan Tru, Sommers, Cavett and I were assigned to Charlie Company. Cavett and I were assigned to the third platoon and Sommers was sent to the first. The three of us began our combat deployments with Charlie Company, 2nd of the 60th Infantry that day at Tan Tru.

16 Tan Tru

Tan Tru was a battalion fire base camp located on rice paddies in the Tan Tru District of Long An Province. Steel walkways on steel barrel foundations, made out of a material called PSP kept feet dry above the flooded rice paddies. When I arrived there the platoon hoochs were wooden structures on concrete filled barrel foundations with canvas covers, like the ones you would see in the TV show and movie M*A*S*H. The base was protected by sand bag bunkers spaced about 150 feet apart with concertina wire and claymore mines out front.

The base consisted of three strait leg infantry companies, Alfa Company, Bravo Company and Charlie Company (and later a Delta Company). A fourth, Echo Company manned 80 mm mortars, and housed the long range patrol (LRRP) platoons. Headquarters (HQ) Company harbored battalion logistics, intelligence, the battalion medic's aid station and the Brass. The tallest structure at Tan Tru was a twenty foot high sandbagged lookout tower manned 24 hours a day by Echo Company. The fire base was also the home of the "C" Battery, 2/4th Artillery which manned a half dozen 105mm howitzer cannons.

The main course infantry operations conducted out of Tan Tru were air mobile assaults called Eagle Flights. There was a dirt road just outside the base camp that led down to the Vam Co River, a tributary of the Mekong, It was long enough to easily accommodate ten or more Huey helicopters and it was used as a helicopter landing and liftoff facility for Air Mobile operations.

A typical Eagle Flight was made up of ten Huey air assault helicopters carrying six soldiers each. This meant that an infantry company had to produce 60 men to man each day's Eagle Flight operations The choppers each had crew chief door gunners on each side. With the pilot and co-pilot up front each ship carried a total of ten men.

The Mekong Delta had large, wide swaths of open rice paddies framed by wood lines that surrounded its waterways. This terrain provided plenty of open room to insert ten helicopters into landing zones almost anywhere. The Delta was literally infested with Viet Cong enemy that used the waterways for transport and the adjacent wood lined jungle for cover.

Hopping aboard a Huey was a rush. Ten helicopters lined up with rotors flying on the pick-up zone put out some serious noise. Back at Fort Polk we trained by jumping off rusted Huey fuselages sitting on blocks. We were taught to jump from them on a call from a trainer's whistle and find cover and wait for orders to move out.

The real thing was dramatically different. Boarding a cranked up Huey in real combat was an assault on the senses. Even before lift-off the ships rocked as the engines idled. We looked out through the front windows and gazed on the dash board gauges between the helmets of the pilots as we rocked on the pad getting ready for take-off. The pilots nodded to each other waiting to crank up the rotors, tip forward and slide upward.

When the moment came the Hueys would rev up, bounce softly, leave the ground, pitch forward and take for the sky. It was a power trip. Two pilots, two door gunners and six fully armed infantrymen heading out in ten helicopters flying in formation to fight it out Viet Cong hiding out in the wood lines and river marshes below.

There I was, a teenager with a grand total 135 days of military training under my belt, riding out with a company of infantrymen in one of ten helicopters into combat, doors open, wind blowing through the open choppers at 2500 feet before circling down toward the rice paddies and down to the steaming jungle below. It felt like we were a pretty bad ass, nasty bunch of Americans.

The Huey air assault helicopters were called "slicks". On an Eagle Flight ten slicks would swoop down to insert a company of sixty men, touching down on the rice paddies less than 100 feet from the adjacent wood lines. On the ground we would tumble out of the choppers and take immediate cover behind the closest rice paddy dikes as the slicks flew away. From our positions we would organize and head into the wood lines in search of the enemy.

In many, if not most cases we found small, camouflaged, one person mud packed, covered foxhole type bunkers on the outer edges of the wood lines. If no VC were found we would destroy the individual bunkers using hand grenades.

When each search was completed we would move back out to the open paddies to await pick up by the slicks to be flown to another landing zone. It was not uncommon to make five or six air assaults in a single day of Eagle Flight operations, and there were often times when we would engage the VC in small arms fire at different locations on the same day.

The insertion part of the Eagle Flight operation was the most frightening for me. Many times our landing zones were "hot" as we took ground fire coming in. We could hear the distinctive pop of the AK 47 rounds above the rotor noise of the Hueys, but could do nothing but sit and wait to get on the ground.

We had to be careful about bailing out of the slicks too quickly too, since the pilots always had the option of aborting the insertion. Any man who hopped out too soon could find himself alone on the ground surrounded by VC.

Typically we would be inserted into an area and then head out on company sized (60 men) patrols. Our encounters with the enemy almost always happened with the enemy opening fire on us as we patrolled, spread out heading into or along the sides of the wood lines.

The VC would open up on us with automatic AK-47 weapons fire and we would dive for cover behind the nearest rice paddy dikes. From there we returned fire and shot it out with them, calling in artillery fire and even close support air strikes. Many times we would bring in the artillery fire within one or two hundred feet of our own position, and sometimes even closer. Supporting air strikes dropping 250 pound high explosive (HE) bombs would literally shake the ground beneath us, and seven inch sized chunks of shrapnel would rain down as we took cover behind the paddy dikes.

After a while, when the shooting would finally stop, we would check for wounded and bring in medevac dust offs if needed. Then eventually we would be ordered up to sweep the wood line, an always unnerving proposition. Spread out laterally we would exchange sideways glances with our squad and platoon brothers as we approached each wood line together after each firefight, hoping to God Almighty that any VC there were either dead or gone away.

Once we penetrated the wood line we would round up any weapons and supplies found and survey the damage. Many times we found dead water buffalos and pigs, burning straw huts along with dead or wounded Viet Cong.

Sometimes we would take in captured enemy VC. They would be handcuffed with plastic ties, placed on Hueys, and flown in to division for interrogation and internment as POW's. I always made it a point of lighting a cigarette for these captives. They would be standing in black silk shorts, bareback, covered with Mekong Delta mud and trembling in fear. Sometimes some soldier might slap one of them around in anger, but when I came upon them I would offer them a smoke and a pat on the back. As far as I was concerned they were no longer my enemy. For them the war was, for now at least, over.

17 Combat Infantry Duty

Arriving in the slicks back at Tan Tru after the day's Eagle Flights we would be fed dinner in the battalion mess hall. After dinner we saddled up in our gear once again and prepared for night duty, which was either manning a four person listening post (LP) a couple hundred meters outside the battalion perimeter, going out on a 12 man night ambush patrol (AP), or if you were lucky, pulling perimeter bunker guard.

For night APs and LPs we waited for our eyes to adjust to the dark outside in a staging area after sunset and then we would spread out and head out in a line on foot through the rice paddies toward our assigned destination. On a typical AP we would go out two or three klicks (kilometers) where we set up in three groups of four. We often set up with the middle group at the corner of two dikes with the other groups out thirty or forty feet from the center group.

We would set out Claymore mines in front of our positions and set in for the night. Each four man group had a Starlight Scope, the night vision devices used back then. Each man would pull guard at each position for one hour while the other three slept behind the dike in the paddy. If it was wet season we slept in a few inches of water or mud. In dry season we slept on the dry lumpy ground atop dead rice straw. Over the course of eight hours through the night each man pulled guard twice. If we happened to spring an ambush on VC walking by during the night we would call in reinforcements from Tan Tru along with helicopter gun ships to provide air support if available or artillery.

On most mornings, when no VC had happened past our ambush point, we picked up and hiked back spread out in to base camp for breakfast. After breakfast we were able to take a break and stand down for a few hours using this time to clean our weapons and ourselves. But we would always be on standby alert for our sister battalion, the 2/39th that operated out of another base camp much like ours at Rach Kien twenty or thirty klicks away.

Ninety percent of the time this meant that by early afternoon we would be ordered out to the LZ to hop on the slicks again and fly out to back up the 2/39th, locked up in contact with VC some place. The 2/60th and the 2/39th did the same things, only on alternating days. We were always backing each other up.

This was the way it went seven days a week, on duty day and night in this unrelenting pattern. After a while we only knew the day of the week because each Monday the platoon medic passed out the weekly malaria pills.

Humping through the Delta involved walking over dry, cracked, clumpy dry rice paddies as well as sloshing through deep steaming brown mud marshes. The terrain was affected by the ocean tides which swelled the many canals that connected the rivers and streams and separated the rice paddies from the higher grounds where coconut trees, grasses and Nipa palm shaded thatched straw hooches of small villages built along the waterways. The Vietnamese used the canals to transport rice, fish, and people in wooded sampans.

The receding tides left glistening mud and when we traversed it, with each down step our boots would sink a foot or two down. Pulling each leg out of the mud would leave a large black watery foot print from wet silt sucked up from below the surface. It could be slow going.

The smaller Vietnamese used small logs and thin old wooden planks to bridge the canals whose spans usually ranged from eight to fifteen feet across. The locals were experts at using these small bridges, but it took a bit of experience for larger, American GI's saddled with weapons, ammunition, grenades and combat gear to get the hang of it. But it was surprising how quickly we mastered the art of it. The trick was to keep one's eyes focused on the other side and to keep moving. Stopping mid canal to look down could quickly dump one into the canal in a heartbeat.

Lacking bridges we crossed canals with water up to our necks holding weapons above our heads as we pushed forward, spread out toward our assigned destinations.

Inside wood lines moving through tropical bushes had its own issues. Large red ants often lined branches and simply brushing one would send hordes of the biting insects flying down your sweaty neck. It was not uncommon to see the man in front of you suddenly dropping off gear and tearing off his fatigue shirt as his closest comrade rushed to the rescue swatting off ants with his olive drab Terry cloth towel. The bites hurt like hell and easily raised small welts that took too many minutes to soothe.

All the while each soldier on patrol would be constantly scanning side to side with senses intently alert for the ever present danger of the Viet Cong.

18   Charlie Company

Over in the first platoon Bill Sommers became a regular rifleman, toting an M-16 rifle. In the third platoon Ron Cavett became our squad's grenadier, carrying the M-79 Grenade Launcher. The M-79 was also called a "thoop" gun because of the sound it made when fired. The M-79 launched 40mm high explosive (HE) rounds more than 300 feet, and Cavett quickly became one of the best M-79 guys in Charlie Company. The weapon also fired a shotgun round full of BBs for up close and personal stuff. I was assigned as an ammo bearer for our squad's M-60 machine gunner, John Cleary. Cleary was a sky walking union iron worker from Cleveland, Ohio.

Back in September and October of 1967, when I was just completing basic training back at Fort Ord, about thirty or forty new guys had been assigned to Charlie Company as replacements, just like Cavett, Sommers and I were in February of '68. Cleary had been among them. Cavett, Sommers and I were just about the first replacements the Charlie Company had seen since then, and they were happy to get us.

John Cleary took loving care of his M-60 and it never jammed. The M-60 machine gunner carried three 100 round belts of ammo along with the twenty-three pound M-60. As the assistant gunner/ammo bearer I stayed close to Cleary everywhere we went, toting another three belts (300 rounds) of M-60 ammo Poncho Villa style along with my own M-16 rifle and a dozen loaded magazines of M-16 ammunition that I carried bandolier style. Three or four fragmentation grenades, two canteens of water, a few cans of C-ration, a poncho liner and an olive drab towel pretty much rounded out my gear.

We were fortunate with the caliber of personnel in the third platoon when Cavett and I arrived. Almost all had been in country for five months or more, and there were some great leaders among them. Three of them were promoted to hard sergeant E-5. John Holloway, a mountain boy from Georgia, Ed Crane from Baltimore, and Ed Ryan, a horn rimmed glasses wearer from Colorado. Holloway and Ryan were the squad leaders for the two squads that made up our platoon.

Holloway was in his natural element humping the bushes, and despite the fact that he had already earned two purple hearts he was still fearless. During my first week he decided to groom me to take over the M-60 at some point in the future.

Ed Crane, a dark haired guy with movie star good looks wore a red bandana around his neck out to the field as if to challenge the VC to just try to shoot at him as he walked point day after day. Ed Ryan, the bespectacled professorial type, never lost his cool and always knew what to do in the heat of a firefight, and he was committed to keeping every guy in his squad from doing stupid things.

Cavett and I both felt fortunate to have landed in a platoon with guys like Holloway, Crane, Ryan and Cleary. We had been told back in training to heed the advice of our fellow troopers who had spent some time in country when we reached our assigned units in Vietnam. We were determined from the get-go to learn as much as we could as fast as we could from these guys.

19   A Day in the Bowling Alley

We had experienced some sporadic light small arms fire and a few mortar attacks at Tan Tru from my first days at Tan Tru, but my first major firefight happened sometime around the end of February.

Charlie Company was sent out to the village of An Nuht Tan some ten or fifteen klicks from Tan Tru. It was a tiny village the battalion used on a regular basis from which to conduct operations. Adjacent to the village, which was nestled inside a wood line, was a long open paddy field five or six hundred meters wide and several klicks in length starting from An Nuht Tan, with VC infested deep wood lines on either side. Owing to its shape it was called the "Bowling Alley".

Soon after our arrival Charlie Company ventured out on foot into the Bowling Alley on a company sized patrol. I had not been on line on patrol with the entire company before and I was struck by the picture before me of sixty men patrolling on foot. I took some comfort in the large number as my previous patrols were just platoon size twelve man events.

At about two klicks into the Bowling Alley a booby trap grenade buried in a dike blew two guys from the First Platoon off a paddy dike about five feet into the air. They were about 150 feet ahead of me and Cleary. They had been walking the dike instead of humping the paddies and they paid the price. The dikes were where the booby traps were and if you had any sense you humped out in the paddies. Walking the dikes was easier, but in my opinion you had to be stupid or lazy to use them.

It was the dry season though, and the grenade was buried deep enough into the dry hardened mud of the paddy dike that it only injured the two men. They had both had shrapnel in their legs, but they would be okay. Dumb, stupid luck…and odds were that they would both be off the line for a good while, if not forever.

After we dusted them off we headed deeper into the Bowling Alley a few more klicks to a point where the open paddies narrowed to just a couple hundred feet wide at its terminus at a river. Here the nipa palm and tree canopy along the river was thickening. We crossed through a narrow wood line into an open area about the size of a football field with a dense wood line adjacent to a fairly large river that was about 400 feet wide. All of a sudden we started getting some sporadic AK-47 fire that was more harassment than accurate.

We patrolled up to the wood line next to the clearing where I spotted the wet footprints a VC had left in the mud of a damp marsh. The footprints went into the wood line toward the river. After I reported the foot prints to our platoon sergeant, Sergeant Clark, he told me to follow them into the wood line to check it out. Clark was a black career non commissioned infantry Sergeant First Class E-7 who had been sent to Vietnam with eighteen years in the army under his belt. He was just two years away from retirement and had no interest in getting killed in Vietnam.

When he instructed me to go into the bushes by the river to check it out I responded without much hesitation to Sergeant Clark that I was not about to go into that wood line alone looking for the VC. I was expecting to be reprimanded, but instead he looked at me and just laughed. He said, "Well damn. I guess that means you're not crazy Brooks. I wouldn't go in there either".

A moment later Sergeant Holloway, who had listened to our conversation a few steps away, walked up and said he was going in there to "get that little bastard".

Everyone took a knee and waited as Holloway went in. He was about 25 feet into the wood line when we heard Holloway pulling off a few rounds from his M-16. Seconds later he emerged from the wood line carrying the VC's AK-47. Then he yelled out, "the bastard jumped into the river". Without hesitation several of us ran behind Holloway back into the wood line past a spot where the VC had been. He had left a cooking pot half filled with still warm rice and his field belongings.

We got to the riverside and tossed grenades after the guy, who by this time was probably long gone down stream. None of us fired a shot, and after a few minutes we moved back toward the opening. On the way back out I stopped at the place where the VC was camped out. Looking down at his little encampment I found the VC's wallet lying next to his warm aluminum rice pot. I picked it up and looked through its contents. Inside it held a grainy black and white picture of a young pretty Vietnamese girl holding a little child. It was obviously the guy's wife and child.

We came back into the clearing a couple of minutes later and the company spread out on line and carefully headed toward the wood line to our left that ran perpendicular to the river. We settled there for about five minutes wondering what was going on.

Then we picked up and moved forward along the river toward the next dike. We were about 150 feet away from a wood line up ahead in prone positions when we were opened up on by a huge barrage of AK-47 automatic weapons fire from the wood line.

The entire company dropped to prone positions, and from behind a dike and I fired off a few rounds from my M-16 before scrambling around to collect M-60 ammo from the rest of the squad, then I snapped four or five belts on to Cleary's M-60. The firefight lasted about five minutes. When the fire stopped we stayed behind the dike as Charlie Company's artillery forward observer called in about thirty or forty rounds of 105 mm artillery on to the wood line.

After about 25 minutes we were ordered up and into the wood line, spread out in line. We carefully entered it without incident. We were surprised that the wood line was only about 40 feet wide, and even more surprised that we found absolutely nothing there. With some sense of relief we exited out the other side into another dry, open rice paddy with a dike about 100 feet away.

The entire company had pretty much made its way across the open paddy to the dike only to find a platoon of guys from our battalion's Alpha Company crouched down on its other side. Most of us at our squad level were not even aware that Alpha Company was patrolling in that area. We started to ask them what they were doing there, but before they could respond a barrage of AK-47 automatic weapons fire opened up behind us from the wood line we had just walked through. So now we were down with a platoon from Alpha Company firing back into the wood line we thought we had just cleared.

We hit the ground returning fire in an intense firefight that went on for several minutes. Then I heard over the radio we had wounded and a dust off was being called in. The firing had calmed down when a Huey medevac was touching down about 250 feet behind our position. Just as it came in four or five guys frantically ran toward it carrying a wounded soldier, who looked to be unconscious, his arms and legs limp. The VC began firing at them as they ran toward the dust off. We returned fire to help cover them. They got the wounded guy aboard and it swung up and away.

The firing stopped and Alpha Company's radio squawked up ordering them to another open paddy about 120 meters to our rear for pick up and extraction via a lift of Huey slicks. It was only when the Alpha Company guys picked up and hustled back toward the pick up zone that we saw that they had a KIA.

He was lying face up behind the dike about twenty feet away from me. Then two guys went over to him and were trying to carry him with them, but they could only make it about twenty or thirty feet at a time due to his weight. So I went over to help. He was a big guy, over 6 feet and a couple hundred pounds. Looking down at his face and blond hair I imagined him to be some big farm boy from the Midwest, and I was struck by the knowledge that right now his loved ones back home didn't yet know of his fate.

We were soon ordered back to the pick up zone after Alpha Company was extracted to head back to Tan Tru without sweeping the wood line again, and word quickly spread that the guy that had been dusted off was Charlie Company's company commander (CO) that day. He had been shot through the neck. I was too new in the company to even know his name. I later found out he had been a First Lieutenant.

A little while later we were picked up. As we lifted off in the Huey's we lit up smokes, drank water from our canteens and flew back to Tan Tru in silence. As we flew back I thought about the dead guy and about Danny Powell back at Fort Hood, and what lay ahead for him when he made it over here with his battalion in another month or so.

20 Losing Hearts and Minds

In March of 1968 the American forces in Vietnam were going balls out after the enemy throughout Vietnam. In the wake of the Tet Offensive they drove us night and day. We continued our pattern of Eagle Flights and night ambush patrols and we were out every day and we slept in rice paddies every night.

With exception of the Mobile Riverine Force (MRF) Brigade which undertook combat operations off of Navy ships, in the Mekong Delta the army operated out of base camps to which we returned after brief operations in order to allow our feet to dry out to prevent what the army called immersion foot.

Even during the dry season soldiers in the field forged through marshes of brackish mud and crossed streams on foot holding weapons and ammo above our heads as we crossed. We all carried an extra pair of socks, changing often in the field, drying out the wet ones by tucking them inside our jungle fatigues.

In March the three main companies of the 2/60th were in numerous firefights, as were the other battalions of the 9th Infantry Division throughout the Delta. In virtually every instance the VC initiated contact with us as we patrolled spread out throughout the paddies and wood lines of the Delta.

We encountered dozens of Vietnamese villages where our presence would set off shouting, and I presumed cursing, by the locals as we searched their hootchs for weapons and enemy materials. The shouting always came from women, as there were never any men (well, young men) around. At the center of every hooch in the delta was a family sized mud bunker with two foot thick walls where the family could take refuge during the firefights that broke out around them.

Although we tried to treat the locals with respect we knew that many of them supported the Viet Cong. They must have been pissed off that we never failed to fill our canteens from the drinking water ceramic pots at the sides of their hooches they captured from rain water. I suspect many despised us for this alone.

21   Vicious Cycle

It didn't take long for me to figure out the war was a major cluster fuck. By my second week in the field I arrived at the conclusion we were never going to win this war. We went out into the field and got into firefights, cleared the wood lines, blew up their bunkers and we left. The ground we gained was given right back.

We were fighting with the same infantry tactics used in World War II, albeit with better equipment and helicopters. But the tactics were the same. Fight the enemy and defeat them on the ground. But the catch in Vietnam was there was no goal to take real estate and neighboring sanctuary countries were off limits. We were stuck in a cycle of fighting that went nowhere, accomplished nothing and never ended.

The VC owned the landscape and we never took it away from them. We shed American blood and gave the land right back to the enemy. It was clear that whatever we were doing was not directed toward winning. The politicians back in Washington were locked into a war plan to wear the North Vietnamese down by killing them off to a point where they would give up and stay home. But in the Mekong Delta they were already home.

Eighty percent of the population of South Vietnam lived in the Mekong Delta, and the Viet Cong warriors there had only to sink back into their hamlets or cross the border into Cambodia to regroup and come back after us when it was to their tactical advantage. I believed then as I do now that our goals in Vietnam were noble. But there is nothing more futile than fighting an enemy where we restricted our forces.

There was no way we were going to send ground forces into North Vietnam or into Cambodia and Laos to destroy them and end this nightmare. It was a stalemate. And even though we grunts on the ground rarely talked it over between ourselves, we all knew what was happening and we understood that this war was about personal survival for twelve months, and we all fought like hell for each other to keep ourselves and our comrades alive. We hated the VC because they were trying to kill us and we tried our best to kill them to preserve our own lives and the lives of our fellow soldiers.

So we soldiered on together surviving as best we could one day at a time. Hopping on the slicks, hitting landing zones, humping the paddies, eating C-rations, sleeping on the rice paddies, pulling APs and LPs, calling in sit reps at fifteen minute intervals, searching hamlets, blowing bunkers with fragmentation and concussion grenades, fighting off red ants and mosquitoes, cleaning our weapons and dreaming of the great silver dust off that was a DC 8 airliner that might someday carry us each home and out of the shithole that was Vietnam.

Well into my second month in Vietnam I thought about Danny Powell and George Vander Dussen still back at Fort Hood, Texas in training. I felt sorry for what lie ahead for them. I hoped they were being well trained but I already understood that surviving Vietnam as an 11 Bravo was as much a matter of luck as it was training.

Sitting on my cot inside our platoon tent one afternoon at Tan Tru, while we were on back up standby for the 2/39th I wrote a letter to Danny to try to give him a picture of what Vietnam was like. I tried to be optimistic throwing in phrases like "a guy can get through this if he keeps his head down and avoids unnecessary heroics".

A couple weeks later a letter from Danny arrived. He told me he and George were home on leave and had their orders for Vietnam. They would be in country by around

March 26th. They were coming over together as a unit of the 198th Light Infantry Brigade (LIB) and they were headed for somewhere up in the northern part of South Vietnam.

22 The Pink Palace

Toward the end of March Charlie Company began conducting a new kind of operation the higher ups called a "Bushmaster". It was the dry season and we could stay in the field for longer stretches of time because the paddies were pretty dry and we could conduct operations without having our feet submerged in the Mekong Delta mud and brackish waters for longer periods.

I had a pretty low opinion of the tactics we mostly employed, namely hitting five or six landing zones in a day where we were sometimes inserted no more than fifty feet from the VC bunkered in on the edge of the wood lines. The brass seemed to feel we could drop right on top of the VC and assault their sorry asses. In truth the opposite was true. We were sitting ducks coming in by chopper right in front of them. The battalion commanders and the brigade commanders could fly around in their command and control (CC) choppers high above and watch from a safe distance while we got shot at coming in.

I always felt better approaching any situation on foot. My two feet were never going to take me where I refused to go. Not so with the slicks. They controlled where you went right up to the point where you jumped off of them.

In a Bushmaster five or ten choppers would insert us into a rice paddy somewhere, after which we would clear the wood line like every other air assault. But when they came to extract us 35 or 40 minutes later only two soldiers would board the slicks; one sitting in the open doorway on either side as they lifted off. This gave the appearance to the VC that all had been extracted. The remaining forces on the ground would take cover quietly in the wood line for as long as twenty-four hours before moving out to set up ambush positions.

I thought it was a smart tactic, and the VC in the area had no idea we were still in the area. On more than one Bushmaster we encountered VC roaming freely about and we were able to engage them on our terms.

Nearing the end of March, 1968, about the time Danny Powell and George Vander Dussen were arriving in Vietnam with their unit from Fort Hood, Charlie Company hiked out of a Bushmaster along Highway 4, one of the main routes through the Mekong Delta, to a place that quickly became known as the Pink Palace.

The Pink Palace was a large, abandoned brick and pink stucco building with two or three accessory structures on a couple of acres next to the highway. Some said it had once been a rice experimental facility built and operated by the French when that country had ruled Vietnam when it had been a part of French Indo-China.

When we arrived there it was long abandoned and all its structures were pock marked by artillery, mortar and small weapons damage. The structures had modern plumbing with tiled bathrooms inside the buildings with ceramic flush toilets that had long gone inoperative.

When we came upon the Pink Palace Charlie Company had been in the field on an operations for about four weeks. For that entire time we had eaten nothing but C-Rations. Over this period we had conducted dozens of Eagle Flights and several Bushmaster operations from different locations throughout Dinh Tuong and Long An Provinces without returning to Tan Tru, spending every night in the field on ambush patrols or Bushmasters. As a consequence, we had gone without so much as a shower or a change of laundry for the entire time. To describe each of as "ripe" would have been a gross understatement.

There was a small, shallow reservoir there created by an old five foot high rock and cement dam. We used it to bathe ourselves with the clothes still on our backs with bar soap. It felt wonderful.

Across Highway 4 from the Pink Palace was a large expanse of open rice paddy land, yellowed with dry rice straw covering hardened, clumpy mud. Behind the Pink Palace was a thick wood line less than five hundred meters back with several hooches tucked inside. It was a designated "free fire zone" back there, an area into which we were permitted to test fire weapons at six pm each evening for a "mad minute" when more than 100 soldiers lined up and fired away into that wood line.

We expected to be shortly air lifted back to Tan Tru but we were instead told we would be staying at the Pink Palace for awhile. The first couple of days there we made perimeter improvements with small sand bagged defensive positions. Alpha and Bravo Companies arrived a day or two later and within a week the place was transformed into an auxiliary base camp for three companies of the 2/60th.

The brass took over the Pink Palace building, and a crude field mess area was set up for serving hot chow in the evening that was flown in from Tan Tru. The large open paddy area across Highway 4 became our helicopter landing and pick up zone.

Tan Tru was in Long An Province. It was an area of operation (AO) that held some familiarity for our battalion and an area where the battalion had, at least for the time being, cleared a lot of the VC out. The Pink Palace, we learned, was in Dinh Tuong Province, a few klicks from the City of My Tho, not far from Dong Tam, and deeper south into the Delta. It was an entirely unfamiliar area of operation for the 2/60th. Right from the start we made frequent contact with the VC on patrols there, both on night APs and on full company patrols into the lands behind the Pink Palace.

23   Hot Landing Zone

In the early afternoon of March 31st we went out across the road to the helicopter pick up zone for Eagle Flights. We were to go out in lifts of only five slicks at a time instead of the usual ten because the jungles were thicker and the paddies smaller in the landing zones the brass had mapped out for us that day. Half of Charlie Company's sixty man assault would go in first, and the second lift of five choppers would immediately return to the Pink Palace to get the next thirty.

That day our platoon drew the assignment to fly in the first lift, and six guys of my squad were assigned to the lead chopper, among them were Sergeant Holloway, John Cleary my M-60 boss, Ed Ryan and Ron Cavett.

On Huey slicks they kept large stainless insulated cold water jugs on the floor centered behind the pilot seats. The side doors were either wide open or removed from the slicks and on Eagle Flights two members of the squad sat on the chopper floor with feet dangling outside while the other four squad members sat on a canvas bench seat facing the water jug.

Two door gunners with hanging M-60s sat in notched out enclaves on either side behind the bench seat. On this Eagle Flight I was seated second from the right on the bench seat, M-16 between my legs, butt resting on the floor, barrel pointed skyward for the flight.

As our flight lifted off we gained the usual 2500 foot altitude and headed toward our destination. Flying around up there the air was beautifully cooler and the winds flowing through the chopper made for a wonderful break from the constant heat and humidity of the paddies and jungles at ground level below.

We rarely flew directly to the assault landing zone knowing that the VC below were watching the skies above. There was always a point when the Eagle Flight got serious. The slicks would gain some speed, turn direction and start their descent with a purpose. When this happened we knew we would be on the ground within four to five minutes.

Everyone would double check weapons and survey the ground below to get an idea of what might be down there. At about three hundred feet the door gunners would grab handles and place thumbs on their butterfly triggers. At about 100 feet up the slicks would begin to pitch backwards slowing down for landing.

On this mission when we were only 25 feet above ground we first heard the crack of automatic weapons fire coming into the chopper. The LZ was hot. The door gunners on both sides of our ship opened up as we came in. As lead ship we were headed to a spot only 50 or 60 feet from the wood line in front of us, and our pilot quickly realized the automatic weapons fire from the ground was coming directly from our front, and it was intense.

Instead of putting the ship down right in front of the enemy fire he pitched the helicopter back to a point that it was flying nearly vertical to the ground with the rear rotor tail literally chopping up rice straw grasses coming up from the paddy dike.

The co-pilot flying our helicopter that day had the words "Top Tiger" written on the back of his helmet, and sitting behind him I remember looking at those words as we were coming down in to the LZ. Inside the chopper sitting on the canvas bench while flying in this vertical position I watched green tracers come up through the floor and out the roof about 12 inches in front of me. VC automatic weapons fire was coming right into the exposed underbelly of the chopper.

All of a sudden I felt something like a slap stinging me on the left side of my face. I had no doubt that I had been shot. It was strange how I felt then as I believed for that short moment that I had been shot in the head and I was going to die. I felt a strange peace and serenity and I almost smiled to myself as I waited for darkness that I felt would most certainly come.

I waited to die for several seconds as the chopper descended. When it finally dawned on me that I was not going to die after all, I reached up to my face and felt some kind of a piece of metal sticking out a half inch left of my nose and an inch and a half below my eye. I pulled it out, looked at it when I suddenly realized we were in the process of landing. As we came to the ground I threw the chunk of metal angrily to the floor of the chopper and followed the rest of my squad out of the chopper and down to the rice paddies. The pilots on that chopper did an incredible job in getting us down safely that day.

As soon as we were out the choppers lifted off, up and away. There was some sporadic fire from our guys on the ground for a couple of minutes but that was all. The VC broke off contact as soon as we put troops on the ground. Ours was the only ship that had taken fire as we came in, but we had plenty of descriptions of what our ship looked like coming in from guys in the ships behind us.

As I leaned back on a paddy dike gathering myself and my emotions I realized that I was bleeding badly from the wound on my face. It looked much worse than it was and I could hear a few guys in my platoon telling others that "Brooks is fucked up pretty bad". As it turned out I was the only one in my squad that was injured. It is hard to believe that none of us were killed or seriously hurt with the volume of fire that passed through that chopper.

As I sat there our platoon medic, Clarke Sherff, a Pasadena, California guy came over and placed a small field dressing on me and instructed me to wait for the next lift to come in bearing the rest of Charlie Company, and to hop on to the closest chopper.

Doc Sherff told me he would follow me carrying my gear. About ten minutes later the next lift were inserted about 150 meters away. I jogged over to them beating Doc Sheriff by about 100 feet. I needed stitches and I was to be flown over to the 3rd Surgical Hospital at Dong Tam. Doc handed me my M-16 and tossed the rest of my gear on to the floor of the chopper after me.

Lifting off I sat alone in the center of the canvas bench seat and gazed down at the Delta below. It was only about a fifteen klick ride to Dong Tam and as we descended and approached the sprawling base we passed over a large swimming pool at about 200 feet. As I looked down at the swimmers and loungers below I could hear the Beach Boys music over the thumping noise of our helicopter. I thought to myself at that moment that I had a pretty shitty MOS.

When we landed on the chopper pad next to the Third Surgical Hospital the emergency personnel met me at the chopper pad and asked me if I was the head wound patient. By the serious expressions on their faces I could tell they were expecting a very seriously wounded patient. I was confused by the question and I answered "I don't think so". I was quickly brought into an air conditioned Quonset building lined with hospital beds on two sides.

I was the only patient there. They sat me down on the second bed next to the entry door and a physician looked at my injury. He told me they would clean my wound and that I would be getting a couple of stitches.

A couple of minutes later as I waited another helicopter touched down outside and a half a dozen emergency medical personnel ran out to meet it. Moments later they brought a guy in on a stretcher and placed him on the bed next to me. They began working frantically on him cutting away clothing, inserting an IV into his arm.

It was apparent right away that this guy was the "head wound" patient they had been expecting when I arrived. He was unconscious but still alive and he had a traumatic bullet wound in the head. As they worked on him I heard the head trauma physician tell the others that they would be unable to treat him there. They were trying to somehow stabilize his condition and call for another medical helicopter to transport him to another hospital.

Sitting on the next bed watching this unfold I began to feel light-headed. When one of the nurses stepped back and looked at me I asked her if it was ok if they moved me to the other side of the ER away from where I was sitting, and she immediately walked me down to another bed on the other side.

Fifteen minutes later they carried the guy out to the helicopter pad and had him on his way. Then the doctor came over and treated me. I was given two stitches and had a bandage placed over the cut. They told me that I had been hit with a ricochet round that had been slowed sufficiently so that it failed to penetrate my head. After getting a tetanus shot I was released and cleared to return to my unit the next day. My platoon medic could remove my stitches in about five or six days.

I left the medical unit and found my way to an Enlisted Men's (EM) Club where I sat down alone and drank a couple of beers and allowed the day's events to begin to sink into my brain.

That night I stayed in the medical barracks for transits at the Third Surgical Unit. Before I sacked out I listened on Armed Forces Viet Nam Radio (AFVN) to a nationwide address by President Lyndon B. Johnson. In that speech the President announced he would not run for and he would not accept the Democratic nomination for another term as President of the United States.

It was March 31, 1968, probably the reason I have remembered the date all this happened.

24 Machine Gun Time

The next morning, on April 1st, I caught a re-supply deuce and a half out of Dong Tam for the Pink Palace, where I was welcomed by the guys of the third platoon. We all talked about the previous day's events and then Cleary took me aside and made a personal announcement. He was getting off the line. He had been on the line since September and the CO gave him some job in supply or something. Then he presented me with his M-60. I was now the squad's machine gunner. I was also given orders for a promotion to Specialist Four (E-4) on that day. I had been in the army for a grand total of eight months.

As I said before, Cleary's M-60 was a good one and it never jammed. You could run grass and straw through it on the belt and it chewed it up and kept going. Since I was now to be the squad's machine gunner, there were a couple of guys who wanted my M-16 because it was one of the newer models with a closed end flash suppressor.

Some of the older model M-16s had a tendency to jam. They also had open ended flash suppressors at the end of their barrels that could get caught on hanging vines in the bush. I don't remember who got my M-16 but I do remember that when I handed it over it had a lot of my blood caked on it from the previous day.

That afternoon Ed Ryan pulled out a Purple Heart medal he had stuck away some place and pinned it on me as I stood at attention in a mock ceremony next to our squad's bunker at the Pink Palace, and someone took my picture for the event.

I figured that becoming a machine gunner for the squad was not such a bad deal. I had no desire to become a hero and humping the M-60 would preclude me from having to walk point. The guys who walked point, whether it was for a squad, platoon or the company were the heroes as far as I was concerned. Walking point was the most dangerous thing a guy could do, and those who did so not only had to have great instincts as to where they led the unit and extremely keen senses, but they had to have confidence and incredible courage. I was a big guy, at six feet two, and strong enough to carry the gun. And I was a city kid who wanted nothing to do with walking point.

So now I needed an assistant gunner to be assigned to me. Sergeant Holloway asked me if Van Etsitty might be all right. Etsitty had been in country much longer than me, since October. He was a quiet, soft spoken Navajo Indian from Gallup, New Mexico. I didn't know much about Van but we became very close over the next couple of months. He was already 29 years old, the oldest guy in the squad, having been drafted when he was 28, and he was a Mormon. He was one of those guys that never complained. He just did his job as a rifleman in the platoon.

Etsitty could not drink alcohol. During the one or two times I persuaded him to have a beer with me he became totally intoxicated on a single beer. He was a full blooded Navajo and his system just could not handle booze. I was surprised to find out he was a Mormon because he didn't fit the profile in my mind of a Mormon. I figured the Mormon Church had missions in New Mexico and Etsitty was one of the Navajos who had joined the faith.

A machine gunner and his ammo bearer become inseparable in combat and Etsitty was one of the best at what he did. A couple of days after I became the M-60 guy Charlie Company was hit while on a company sized patrol a few klicks behind the Pink Palace, near the area where our helicopter hit the hot LZ on March 31st. As we took cover behind the dike to return fire Etsitty had 400 rounds of ammo snapped onto my gun within the first 30 seconds.

I was gaining important experience fast in those early months in Charlie Company. When I first arrived I knew that I had twelve months of very dangerous duty ahead of me. But, I refused to allow myself to believe that I would not get through it. I guess the mind kind of takes over when one is in situations like that and I figure soldiers in every war experience a similar kind of mental phenomenon to deal with it.

In my case I simply refused to accept that I could be hurt, let alone killed in Vietnam. Call it a faith that God will protect you or a refusal to accept reality. Whatever it was I forced myself to believe in my personal invulnerability. It was the only way I could cope with the situation. This didn't mean that I was taking foolish chances for I certainly did not. But it helped get me through the early weeks there. Everyone knew that the first couple of months in combat there were the most dangerous.

After March 31st I had to mentally readjust. Even though I was not seriously wounded my personal sense of invincibility was shattered. I fully understood that we had been incredibly lucky to come away from the hot LZ as well as we did.

One of the ways I reacted was to become much angrier. It was not intentional. It was just the way it was. With each firefight I became more jumpy and in the wake of each instance of getting shot at I felt more rage toward the VC. I had also developed what psychologists call a startle response wherein I would flinch at the sound of gun fire or any loud noise remotely resembling it. Most of the other guys in the squad developed that same thing too.

At the conclusion of that first firefight following March 31st, with the machine gun behind the Pink Palace we crossed a canal with a sampan with two elderly Vietnamese lying dead inside. They had been killed by our artillery during the firefight. There was a hooch behind the canal, and I was the first guy into it as Charlie Company was inside the wood line searching and clearing it out. There was also a line of small VC bunkers along the canal that were in the process of being blown up.

As I approached the hooch I found there were about two hundred expended AK-47 shells in the threshold of the front doorway. Walking inside I found two women, one young, one old sitting by and staring down at a table. They were just sitting there as if nothing happened and they were knitting.

At six foot two, carrying that big machine gun, sweating like a pig, with a bandage next to my nose and still sporting a black eye from my injury I must have looked like a giant ogre to those tiny little women. I yelled at them in English asking them what was with those AK-47 shells in their doorway, and where were the fucking VC? They just sat their staring down at their knitting saying nothing, ignoring me, just knitting.

In a rage I walked out the front door and pulled the bamboo supports away from the front of the hooch, collapsing the roof halfway down to the ground. The two women scrambled out the back door as I lit the roof on fire with a chunk of C4.

As we left the wood line that day hiking back to the Pink Palace I looked back and watched as that hooch, empty of its occupants, was burning to the ground.

25 A New Platoon Leader

There was radio in Vietnam and plenty of guys had ghetto blasters to listen to the only station. AFVN Radio carried the news a couple days later of the Martin Luther King Jr. assassination. There were blacks and Mexicans and an Asian and the rest whites in our platoon, mostly whites. We all heard about racial problems involving blacks in Vietnam, but in line companies like ours they were minimal at best. We were all in the same bucket of shit and we all had way too many other things to think about at the time.

Even the Southern whites and blacks got along. I suppose it was different in rear echelon units but it didn't surface in our unit, at least not during the early part of 1968. Still, King's assassination was an especially sad day for the blacks in our platoon, in Charlie Company and throughout the battalion. Mostly people didn't say anything about it, but it seemed the black guys huddled pretty close together for a while after that. And no one could blame them.

Lieutenant Sargent had long since completed his six month assignment to the field. Field Officers (Lieutenants and Captains) spent six months of their one year Vietnam tour in the field as platoon leaders and company commanders and six months as a staff officer. In early April the third platoon was assigned a new platoon leader. His name was First Lieutenant Peter Campbell.

New platoon leaders in combat units needed to be broken in carefully. The really good ones held back and took advice from experienced NCOs in the platoon for the first month, gradually assuming full leadership of the platoon. I think Lieutenant Campbell tried his best to do this too, but he was way too eager to get into the fight. When he arrived he gathered up the platoon and gave us a little introductory speech. He told us he had already been in country for six months stuck, as he put it, in a damn staff job up at division, and he was itching to get out to the field into battle and kill some Viet Cong.

To a man our reaction in the platoon was a feeling that this guy was an idiot, and we just hoped that after getting a firefight or two under his belt he would wise up and calm down. Our very real concern was that this kind of attitude leading the third platoon could get us killed. But in the Army you had to take what they gave you, and division had just given us Lieutenant Campbell.

His first night as platoon leader Campbell led an ambush patrol. Night ambushes were set up at predetermined locations, but the platoon had some discretion as to where they were actually set up depending on what was encountered in the field. If, for example, we came upon a stream or canal made impassable due to high tides we could set up in an alternate location. Sitreps (situation reports) were called in every fifteen minutes throughout the night so any deviation from the plan was known back at the battalion HQ. But Lieutenant Campbell insisted on taking us three and a half klicks out in the wood lines and the paddies on that first patrol to a destination he himself selected.

It involved way too much night patrolling to get there and it was in an area where a twelve man patrol could easily get itself into a nasty jam. Fortunately we made it out and back without running into Victor Charlie that night, but the experience with our new platoon leader had everyone on edge.

That was the way it kept going for us with Campbell. At least for the first two weeks that he was our platoon leader.

26   April 17th

On the seventeenth of April we went on Eagle Flights out of the Pink Palace. We were heading out somewhere a few kilometers away from Cai Lai, a tiny hamlet located east of the Pink Palace on Highway 4. Charlie Company's first platoon led by Lieutenant Victor Mika went out on the first lift, along with a portion of Bravo Company, as the rest of Charlie Company waited out in the dry paddies across Highway 4 from the Pink Palace to fly out in a second lift. It was a pretty big operation involving a couple of companies in the initial air assaults.

We thought it might be an easy insertion when we noticed First Sergeant Bobo, carrying his trusty M-14 rifle going along out with first lift of choppers. It turned out to be anything like a milk run.

As we waited we monitored the insertion on the PRC 25 radios as we always did. Everyone could hear what was happening because the radios were all set on speaker. As the first lift hit the LZ we monitored the action. They hit a hot LZ and there were casualties right from the start. Once the guys made it onto the ground they were pinned down by heavy machine gun fire only 50 feet or so from the edge of the wood line.

They had come in hot and Bill Sommers was hit in the arm while still in his ship. As it landed he hopped out anyway and took cover behind the first paddy dike just fifty feet from the wood line. Bunkers along the wood line were pouring heavy machine gun and AK 47 fire down on them as well as rocket propelled grenades (RPG).

Right after making it to the dike Sommers heard a loud explosion behind him. It was an RPG explosion and it mortally wounded Lieutenant Mika nearly blowing off one of his legs. He was in shock and he bled to death in the dry rice paddy right there.

The enemy had lined the edges of the wood line with a series of thick mud camouflaged bunkers with AK 47s and AK 50 machine guns. The higher ups had done it again I thought, trying to land the slicks right on top of the wood line instead of further back where troops could probe and approach the wood line more carefully without getting the crap shot out of them in the LZ.

In ten minutes the choppers returned. As soon as they were down the crew chief door gunners hopped down from their mounts, unhooked the communications wires from their helmets, and began surveying the damage to their ships, checking for bullet holes and looking for hydraulic leaks and the like. We had seen this happen many times before, and when you are waiting to hop on those ships for your turn in the barrel it was always unsettling.

We waited for a while as they checked out the damage and finally turned off their engines. I figured that up in the air in the command and control (CC) chopper the battalion commander and back at battalion HQ the brass were discussing the situation and no doubt coordinating with the 2/39th for back up to seal the other side of the wood line and finding a suitable insertion point before ordering the rest of us in.

Then the air crews began to stir. We watched as one by one they hopped up into their ships. A few minutes later they started up their engines and we all knew it was getting close to time to saddle up and mount the helicopters. Extra boxes of M-16 and M-60 ammunition were brought out for us to re-supply the guys still pinned down behind the first dike who were running out of ammo. Everybody carried on as much of it as he could handle.

Finally we boarded the slicks and lifted off. We flew up to the usual 2500 feet and looked out to the paddies, rivers, marshes and jungles below. In the distance we could see smoke rising up from a wood line and we circled that area for almost an hour. We all knew that was where the ball game was going on. I found myself smoking cigarette after cigarette looking down at the smoke knowing we were going to be under fire and hoping we would not get shot up when we hit the LZ.

After awhile we turned downward and began our approach. We were relieved coming in when it became evident they were inserting us well back and away from the edge of the wood line from where the smoke was coming. As we descended a chopper ahead of us laid down a thick smoke screen layer the length of the LZ. I'd never seen this done before that day.

When we landed there was sporadic fire coming at us but it was from a good distance away. All 60 of us on the ground took cover behind dikes and got ready to maneuver our way up across about 500 meters of dry rice paddies up to where the first platoon was pinned down. The ground between us and the wood line in front of them was wide open dry rice paddy. It was about 200 meters wide with a paddy dike running across about every 50 or 60 meters up to the wood line.

Normal tactics would have the guys up front provide fire cover for us as we moved forward from dike to dike or we could cover ourselves with an alternating fire and maneuver tactic. Neither method would work here. The problem was the guys up front were nearly out of ammunition and we could not fire and maneuver either because we had friendlies between us and the bad guys.

So instead we were ordered to move forward under the cover of artillery fire. Our artillery forward observer called in 105mm artillery high explosive rounds right behind the enemy bunkers on the edge of the wood line. The entire company made it forward on line to a dike about eight paddies from the first platoon. Half of the company on line was ordered to advance to the next forward dike as the 105 shells landed. Then the other half would do the same as the next volley of rounds hit, alternating left half-right half. It worked pretty well. The enemy fire stopped as the rounds landed allowing us to move up dike by dike.

The closer we came to the front dike our own artillery shrapnel became a bigger issue. We had to get up and run forward as the shit was flying past us, and the closer we got the deeper I would crouch while trying to run forward. With Etsitty beside me I carried the M-60 like a lunch pail by its handle as I ran. I was wearing three 100 round belts of ammo over my shoulders Poncho Villa style, as was Etsitty, and we were both carrying an extra ammo box in the other hand.

When we were only one dike behind the guys pinned down the artillery came in and we were up and running again. The rounds crunching ahead were deafening and I was crouching even further down as I ran. Half way across the open paddy I stumbled and went sprawling face down. My helmet went rolling one way the ammo box went the other and the M-60 and I lay there for a moment as the artillery momentarily halted.

I heard Specialist Majewski, the company commander's radio operator (RTO) and a former member of the third platoon, yell at me from the dike behind asking if I was hit. I responded that I had only stumbled and he yelled back at me to get up and get up to the dike. They needed the M-60 up there.

So I crawled around and gathered my gear, took a deep breath and got up and ran forward. I made it to the dike with a dive and Etsitty immediately began snapping belts onto my gun as we passed out fresh ammo to the guys up there.

The dike was about two feet high and the enemy had its guns precisely sited on the top. When they fired you could literally see the dry mud fly off the top of the dike as their rounds hit it. By this time I was so angry and fired up that as soon as I opened up with the machine gun I kept firing back at them until I had ran about a belt and a half (150 rounds) nonstop. Etsitty was beating me on my back to stop lest I burn up the gun's barrel. I finally calmed down enough to begin firing in five or six round bursts.

It was a barn burner of a firefight that went on for ten or fifteen minutes before the enemy decided it was time to break it off and get out. It turned out that the wood line was about 200 meters deep and it contained a number of hooches inside it along with pigs and water buffalo. When the firing finally stopped I had fired 900 rounds from the M-60, which left me only 100 rounds remaining. For a few minutes we rested behind the paddy dike drinking water from our canteens when the company commander came over the radio asking who wanted to go into the wood line first. Right on cue Lieutenant Campbell volunteered the third platoon. He even said "Let's go in there like infantrymen!" Upon hearing this I remember thinking that this was not an Audie Murphy movie, and what the hell was Campbell trying to do to us?

This was one of those times I was happy to be carrying the M-60. Heading in first was a rifleman's job so I made my way around to the left side front of the wood line where the guys were going in. Lieutenant Campbell was leading the way, as Etsitty and I took cover behind the dike at the edge of the wood line. Then, after about 90 seconds, shots rang out from 20 meters inside.

It was AK 47 fire coming in our direction with M-16 fire going the other way. After about ten shots it stopped. Then Campbell's RTO's voice cracked over the radio that Campbell was down and we needed an urgent dust-off.

I stayed put at the wood line entrance as the third platoon medic along with Sergeant Ed Ryan went in to treat Campbell as the rest of the company secured the rest of the wood line. When they reached Campbell he had some sort of bullet wound to his cheek and another to a leg around his knee. It took ten or fifteen minutes before a dust off arrived as the medic was treating him, and when it touched down they carried Campbell out on a stretcher and hoisted him into the chopper.

Campbell had made a five dollar bet with one of the men in our squad that the guy would get wounded before Campbell. He looked pretty bad as they lifted him to the dust off and he was not moving. Just before the ship lifted away the soldier yelled to him "you owe me five bucks Campbell!' at which time Campbell's arm lifted up from the stretcher giving the finger.

We were not exactly taken with his style of leadership in the third platoon but it was great relief to all of us seeing him do that, as the chopper lifted off. It was also a bit of a relief that his stint as our platoon leader was over.

Afterwards we patrolled through the wood line to the other side. There were dead enemy soldiers, dead pigs, dead water buffalo, and burning hooches and smoldering piles of rice. Seated in a rice paddy, his back leaning on the dike on the back side of the wood line, was a fully uniformed, dead, North Vietnamese Army (NVA) officer who had been strafed by helicopter gunship fire. So, I thought as I stood there looking down at him, the local Mekong VC were now being assisted by regular North Vietnamese Army (NVA). Welcome to the Delta I thought as I looked down at him.

Twenty feet out on the open paddy there were remains of two more enemy soldiers next to a 105 artillery crater. There was nothing left of the two bodies but trunks. No heads, no arms, no legs.

Later we formed a perimeter around the wood line and spent the night there. The next morning we headed out to the open paddies on the back side of the wood line and readied for choppers to ferry us back to the Pink Palace. But before we left a couple of Hueys came flying in with a CBS News crew, the battalion brass, and some paymasters from division.

In addition to CBS reporters interviewing the brass about the battle the day before, they were actually compensating the Vietnamese owners of the dead water buffalo and pigs, and destroyed property with cash money for the benefit of the news crew. This was a new one.

After this dog and pony show they brought in a big Chinook helicopter and began hauling us back to the Pink Palace. When we had returned there we were told by Captain Cadigan, our company commander, that Lieutenant Campbell lost the injured leg.

It was a rough day for Charlie Company. Two platoon leader line officers lost. Lieutenant Campbell lost his leg and Lieutenant Mika had lost his life.

27 The Gunfighter Takes Over

Early in my tour I tried to write home to my mother as much as I could. But knowing full well the delicate state of her health, I spared her the ugly details of my military activities. I didn't get much mail myself. I had no girlfriend waiting for me back in the states and I was grateful. Lots of guys got one or more letters from sweethearts back home on a daily basis only to see the numbers dwindle over time and finally end with the final letter starting with the words "Dear John". There's nothing like getting dumped by your girl when you are fighting for your survival in a war in a distant land. Terry wrote to me every month. Since my arrival almost three months earlier I had received but one letter from my mother.

Finally, later in April I came in from a patrol to find a letter from Private First Class Danny Powell. Written more than a month earlier it took that much time to travel some three hundred miles to reach me. A letter from the states would arrive in less than a week, but for some reason, in-country soldier to soldier mail could take several weeks.

I was happy to finally hear from Danny, eager to see what he was doing and where he was. He described that he was doing well and he was still in the same platoon with George Vander Dussen. I couldn't figure out where they were exactly, but they were hundreds of miles north of the Mekong Delta. Danny said he was set to be assigned the job of radio operator (RTO) for his platoon leader and though he had been in country for just a couple weeks, he wanted the job because he always wanted to know what was going on.

After reading his letter I sat down and wrote him right back to bring him up to speed as best I could on what was going on with me down in the Mekong Delta.

As it turned out his unit, B Company, 5th of the 46th Infantry, 198th Light Infantry Brigade (LIB) was operating in the vicinity of Cu Chi and near the South China Sea in the I Corp Sector in northernmost South Vietnam.

The unit was new to Vietnam. They had formed at Fort Hood in Texas and were dumped into the Americal Division, a named coined for the 23rd Infantry Division, a unit consisting of brigades serving all over Vietnam, the 199th LIB, the 196th LIB and now the 198th LIB.

Danny Powell (foreground) in Vietnam

I finished the letter and tried to imagine Danny patrolling through jungles up there with a platoon, and a company of newly arrived soldiers from Fort Hood, Texas trying to get a grip on the jungle dangers and North Vietnamese Army enemy coming from just over the Demilitarized Zone (DMV) around the Marine Base at Khe Sanh. I hoped he would be all right.

28 Colonel Henry Emerson and Bushmasters

Lieutenant Campbell had been gone for a couple of weeks, and it was about this same time we were assigned a new platoon leader to replace him. Lieutenant Bill Schmiedecke was a young second lieutenant from Florida. If one could construct an officer who was the exact opposite from Campbell it would be Schmiedecke. He was some kind of a local entertainer in Florida before he was drafted into the infantry.

He had volunteered to attend Officer Candidate School (OCS) following his advanced infantry training to avoid being sent directly to Vietnam. OCS lasted about six months and he figured the longer he could avoid Vietnam the better, and besides he thought it better to go over as an officer than as a PFC.

The men in the third platoon loved the guy. Right from the start he deferred to the experience of the veteran NCOs, like Sergeant Holloway in the platoon, and as far as the VC were concerned he believed it was best to take a live and let live position. Of course, he was prepared to fight like all of us were, but if it could be avoided we would all be better off in the long run.

We soon discovered that the battalion brass and our company commander considered him a pain in the ass. He was regularly late for briefings at HQ and could not have cared less how they felt about him. He understood that the most important thing in Vietnam was to survive a tour and make it home in one piece.

He turned out to be too good to be true. About three or four weeks after he became our platoon leader the brass transferred him out of Charlie Company to a Military Assistance Command Vietnam (MACV) unit.

Sometime in May, the Ninth Division switched the 2/60th from the Third Brigade to the First Brigade. I figured this was mainly an administrative change, in that it did not change the manner in which the battalion operated at all. With the transfer to the First Brigade the 2/60th was also assigned a new Brigade Commander.

His name was Colonel Henry Emerson, AKA "The Gunfighter". Colonel Emerson had a prior tour in Vietnam where he had been a battalion commander with the 101st Airborne Division.

A couple days before he showed up Charlie Arce, a young soldier from Bravo Company I had met, stopped by the our platoon hooch, as we were waiting around on standby to back up the 2/39th, to talk with me about Colonel Emerson. Arce was Mexican kid from Montebello, in southeast LA, not far from Paramount, where I grew up and we had become good friends.

He was a tall good looking guy with a crazy southeast LA Chicano attitude. Somewhere Arce had come into possession of one of those military war story magazines. It had a cover story about Colonel Henry Emerson's "Jump into Hell Commandos" based on Emerson's previous tour as a battalion commander with the 101st Airborne Division two years prior. Arce was wide eyed with wonder about what Emerson held in store for the 2/60th, and I had a few reservations as well, looking over the magazine.

Colonel Hank Emerson has long since been credited with perfecting the Ninth Division's "jitterbug" tactics, in which infantry companies are inserted by helicopter in several locations in a day. When one unit would make contact with the enemy he would quickly bring in other troops by air assault to seal off escape routes in order to kill or capture the enemy forces. To me it was virtually the same thing we had always done with Eagle Flights but under Colonel Emerson's command it was done even more aggressively and with more coordination with other backup battalions.

On the day he visited us at the 2/60th Emerson formed the unit's companies together at the Pink Palace and gave us a personal introduction. Standing before us like General George S. Patton he addressed to the assembled troops. In a rousing speech he encouraged us to raise our heads above the paddy dikes during our firefights and to carefully level and aim our weapons at the Viet Cong enemy, a recommendation met with unanimous agreement that this was one of the silliest recommendations ever espoused by our military leadership, especially ridiculous since we could never actually see any enemy combatants during firefights. At the conclusion of his speech he presented each assembled troop with a black metal uniform pin in the shape of an arrow which he called a "Recondo Pin".

I must admit by this time I, like the rest of the guys in Charlie Company, had little interest in becoming a "Recondo" anything. But I will give it to Emerson. He would soon live up to his "Gunfighter" nickname and he would drive us relentlessly for twenty-four hours a day and seven days a week.

As Brigade Commander Colonel Emerson spent a lot of time flying in a C&C ship. The Army had recently brought over the new Hughes Light Observation Chopper it called the "LOCH". It was a quiet, tiny little helicopter that could buzz around the tree tops and Nipa Palms scouting around for VC. Colonel Emerson spent a lot of time riding around in one doing just that.

We spent the month of May on constant operations. On one single day of jitterbugging we hit eight different landing zones on air assaults. We also continued to conduct bushmaster operations a couple of times, all operating out of the Pink Palace.

On one Bushmaster we were inserted in the early evening. As always the choppers came and pulled off a fake extraction and we settled quietly for the night in an unoccupied wooded area. By the next morning we were lying low on the ground and the enemy in the area had no idea we were there. We moved out quietly through the wood line until we came across an unoccupied hooch with cooking equipment still warm from use. The entrance to the hooch was booby trapped with trip wires hooked to a US Army canteen. It was obvious it was an enemy hooch.

We went around the hooch and quietly made our way across an open paddy where we set up on the edge of another wood line about 500 meters away. We hid there and waited for night fall. At around 2100 hours a cooking fire appeared in the hooch. We knew they were in there.

It was a dark, moonless night and two platoons set out silently, spread out on line in the darkness across the open paddies toward the hooch, stopping at each dike. When we were almost to the final dike before reaching the hooch the fire inside suddenly went out and automatic weapons fire broke out. There were tracers flying in and around the hooch. Curiously, to this point none of us had fired a round but we all hit the deck and began firing into the hooch.

We were caught halfway between dikes in the open paddy firing from prone positions. I was firing the M-60 as a guy from Texas named Hernandez was snapping on belts of ammo. Hernandez was working as my ammo bearer that night because Etsitty was off on his R&R leave. The firing went on for about two minutes before we were told to hold.

None of us could quite figure out what had happened until about ten minutes later when Sgt. Charles Huzico from the other squad in the third platoon yelled "don't shoot!' from his position in a canal cut between the hooch's wood line and the rest of us some 25 meters ahead. It turned out Huzico had decided on his own to become a one man commando and he had secretly gone up ahead of the rest of us up to the hooch all by himself. When he reached the canal he opened up with his M-16.

He was lucky we didn't kill him with friendly fire as we tossed in fire from grenade launchers, full automatic fire from a dozen M-16's and machine gun fire from two M-60's. He had blown the raid because whoever was in the hooch was now long gone in the darkness. The Bushmaster was blown and to top it off Hernandez somehow ended up with a piece of hot shrapnel from one of our own M-79 grenades that pierced though his boot at the ankle.

I never could quite figure out Sgt. Huzico. He was usually very competent and kind of reserved. But he obviously had some kind of impulsive streak.

29 The Plain of Reeds

On the 30th of May a couple of companies including Charlie Company jumped on the choppers and headed out to an area I had heard about called the Plain of Reeds. It was a huge fallow marsh covering hundreds of square miles located just south of the Parrot's Beak, a swath of Cambodia that bulged into the South Vietnamese border northwest of Saigon.

We didn't know it at the time, at least we low ranking grunts, but we were going out there as part of a larger operation that included units of the 1st Infantry Division, the 25th Infantry Division, and the 82nd Airborne Division. All I knew was I hated the place from the get-go. The worst thing was there were no dikes. Dikes were our salvation in the Delta. Without them there was no place to take cover from the enemy that used the densely jungled wood lines along the rivers and canals that ran through the Plain of Reeds.

We were flown out to an isolated Special Forces compound used as a base by a handful of Green Berets who equipped and advised a rag tag company of Cambodian volunteers. The compound was triangular in shape and about an acre in size. There was a high levee like berm protecting it with a filthy, maggot infested canal outside the berm. A small quarter mile long road outside the compound led down to a river. The Cambodian soldiers there looked to be as young as fourteen years old and the old U.S. Army surplus M-1 rifles many of them carried were as long as many of them were tall.

The Special Forces had a quad-fifty caliber machine gun parked out there. It was mounted on a trailer chassis that could be hooked to the back of a jeep. In the first evening there they fired the quad fifty out into the marsh and jungle. The entire Plain of Reeds was considered a free fire zone, meaning you could shoot at anything that walked out there. There were no friendlies on the Plain of Reeds.

The first day there we went out on slicks. We were inserted into a couple of areas near wood lined rivers and swept the areas. In one of the locations we were sniped at from a distance but there was no real heavy fire. We found a couple of AK 47s that had been hastily jammed down in the mud in an effort to conceal and a couple pairs of flip flops left in the mud by fleeing bad guys. During the day's operations out there the absence of dikes or places to take cover was unnerving.

That night we went on an ambush patrol up river from the Green Beret compound. A dozen of us were placed into two small aluminum boats powered by outboard motors that were driven by a couple of Special Forces guys. We set out in the moonlight and went two klicks up the river with thickly wooded banks only fifteen feet from either side of the boats. I could hardly believe we were doing something so stupid. The VC could have blasted us out of the water.

When we reached our destination we set up for ambush on a muddy bank at an open spot next to the river. We didn't ambush anything that night and when we broke and saddled up to return to the compound I was dreading the boat ride back. But we hauled ass back down the river and made it back to the compound that morning without incident.

It was an overcast morning and the humidity almost steamed off the ground as the day began to heat up. We were supplied with Long Range Patrol "LRP" rations out there for chow instead of the normal C-Rations. LRP Rations were dehydrated meals in sealed packets. You had to add water and shake them up to eat them. They were salty and unlike C-Rations one could heat up in a can over a chunk of burning C-4, one needed a pan of sorts to heat LRP Rations. So we were eating our spaghetti or beef stew LRP Rations cold.

I don't remember what I ate that morning but whatever it was I threw it up right after breakfast. As I stood next to a line of sandbags ralphing Sergeant Clark, our platoon sergeant, came up to me and asked me if I was sick and I told him I had an upset stomach. To this day I don't know if it was the LRP Rations or just nerves from being out there, but as the company was saddling up for an Eagle Flight Clark told me to stay back that morning until I was feeling better.

In April Charlie Company was the grateful recipient of a dozen or so new replacements. There were some really good guys among them. One of them was Wayne Pope. He was from Georgia and he was a big guy of about six foot five that I thought might some time take over the M-60 duties from me if I was ever lucky enough to get off the line. So that morning Pope took my machine gun out for me and I held on to his M-16 in return. It felt really strange staying back while the company went out. Since my arrival at Charlie Company I had never missed a day in the field. But it was a strange place on a weird day so I sat down next to a live PRC 25 radio to monitor the insertion and lit up a smoke as Charlie Company lifted off that morning without me for the first time since I arrived at Tan Tru in February.

At Tan Tru

March 1968

In from a patrol and loaded down with a PRC 25 in addition to my other gear with one of our M-79 guys named Castenada. March 1968 at Tan Tru.

Saddled up at the Pink Palace prepared to head out --- May, 1968

From left to right facing camera:

David Carter, Hernandez, John Cleary, and in back, John Holloway.

Edward Ryan and John Cleary

Pink Palace April 1968

Edward Crane and Edward Ryan on the pick up zone (PZ) across Highway 4 from the Pink Palace

April 1968

My Assistant Gunner, Van Etsitty, in May 1968 taking a chow break sitting on a VC bunker.

Van Etsitty took this picture of me with my M-60 Machine Gun and C-rations on a lunch break sitting in a VC Bunker in May 1968.

Edward Ryan popped yellow smoke and is guiding a slick down for pick up

A photo of an adjacent Huey slick taken from my slick on April 17, 1968, heading out in a lift of ten ships into the firefight (smoke below).

Bill Sommers at Tan Tru

Lookout Tower at Tan Tru Base Camp as viewed from
Charlie Company Area

Larry Brooks at the Pink Palace in April of 1968

30   Heartbreak and Shock

Five minutes after Charlie Company lifted off without me the radio cracked with word that the LZ was hot and we had casualties. The Huey carrying my squad with Pope, Etsitty, Ryan, Cavett, Crane and a new fellow, Oscar Phillips, a quiet, 21 year old black kid from Oklahoma City, had landed about ten feet from a VC bunker manned by a guy with an AK 47. He unloaded into the chopper at close range just as it touched down, and before Cavett managed to jump out of the Huey and kill him at point blank range with a shotgun round from his M-79.

Van Etsitty and Oscar Phillips never made it out of the helicopter and they were both badly hurt. They were still inside the Huey as it was returning back to our location. They were calling in another dust off helicopter from some place else to medevac them out that would take fifteen or twenty minutes before it would arrive for them.

In less than five minutes we watched as the slicks returned from the LZ, empty except for Etsitty and Phillips. As the chopper bearing Etsitty and Philips touched down the door gunners jumped down and were helped by several men who met them to carry Etsitty off the chopper. They had no stretcher so four or five carried him, running "face up" by his back, arms and legs to a nearby cot where a field medic was waiting.

As they ran with him past me I saw that his dark Navajo skin had gone nearly blue, and I could see the bloody holes that riddled his jungle fatigue shirt. I knew he was gone.

Oscar Phillips was conscious and a couple of us and a medic helped him from the Huey and carried him over to a makeshift sand bag bunker wall on the road. He was conscious, lucid and he spoke calmly, as he sat down on the sand bags. We quietly offered words of encouragement as the medic lifted his shirt to check his wounds.

He told us he was not feeling any pain but I think he was in shock. While he sat there the medic lifted his shirt and loosened his fatigue trousers to reveal two AK-47 entry wounds in his lower abdomen. We laid him back on an air mattress and the medic gave him a shot of morphine as we waited anxiously for the medevac chopper to arrive. It came after what seemed like an eternity and it took both Phillips and Etsitty out of there.

It was only about an hour later when the assault slicks returned bringing back the remainder of Charlie Company. The guys in my squad filled me in on what had happened out there. It was a somber and pretty rattled third platoon with everyone trying to shake off the shock of the fighting while trying to take in the events.

The troops were quietly cussing out the brass for inserting the company right on top of a wood line again. It was as if the unit commanders thought we could blast away fortified enemy positions by landing the choppers right on top of them. It was stupid. Hueys were not tanks but unit commanders often acted as if they were. I was asked about Etsitty and Oscar Phillips. I told them that Etsitty could not have made it but I was hopeful that Phillips would be okay. Everybody was upset that they didn't fly them directly to a field hospital instead of bringing them back to the Special Forces compound and then waiting for another chopper to come in for them. No one could explain it.

Later in the early afternoon as the squad sat there cleaning weapons Sergeant Clark approached and asked me for my line number. I told him it was 45. Every soldier in the company was assigned a line number when they first arrived. This allowed a soldier's identity to be communicated over the radio without using his name. Then Sergeant Clark said that division had called our company commander over the radio with special orders for Line Number Forty-five.

I had absolutely no idea what this was all about. I walked over to the captain and asked him what this was all about. Then I stood before him in stunned silence as he told me to gather up my gear.

Division had radioed him from Dong Tam. They had priority orders to immediately send me back to the United States on body escort duty.

31   Body Escort Duty

The re-supply helicopter was arriving in about ten minutes, the last one of the day. The captain told me to be on it. I had about that much time to get back over to the third platoon and gather up my gear. Word had already spread back to them that I was going back to "the world". To say it was surreal was a gross understatement.

I didn't have the slightest idea what body escort duty was and everyone wondered if it could possibly have something to do with Van Etsitty. None of us had ever heard of a grunt being yanked out of the field in Vietnam and ordered back to the states on body escort duty. We all said quick good-byes and good luck, and most of them admonished me with "Don't come back, I wouldn't!" And they all meant it.

So late that afternoon I caught a ride on the re-supply chopper headed back in, away from the Plain of Reeds. The chopper was headed toward Dong Tam but they diverted it down to the Pink Palace to drop me off on their way. I needed to pick up my orders there from battalion HQ at the Pink Palace, I was told. From there I could hop a truck into Dong Tam the next day.

Flying back in that afternoon I was confused. I had no idea what this was all about. But I felt elation at the same time. Looking down at the beautiful green rice paddies and rivers of the Mekong Delta below I felt as if I was being plucked out from hell on earth. I was excited, whatever the reason or circumstance, to be getting out of Vietnam if only for a little while. I would deal with the situation when or if I ever returned.

I pulled bunker guard duty at the Pink Palace that night and spoke very little about my situation with anyone. At battalion HQ I was given orders to report to the 9th

Division Graves Registration unit at Dong Tam as soon as possible. Graves Registration, I was shortly to learn, did all of the paperwork associated with processing and shipment of fallen soldiers and, in some cases, the issuance of formal orders for individuals on body escort duty.

I learned it was the duty of the body escort to oversee the transport of the remains of each individual soldier from the military mortuary to the funeral home of the deceased. The body escort also contacted and assisted the next of kin assisting with funeral arrangements if needed, providing life insurance assistance, and attending the funeral and gravesite services. In transit the body escort made certain the body was properly handled and he stood at attention and saluted whenever the box containing the casket was within view during transit, such as loading and unloading for transfer to different forms of transit. It was a solemn duty with utmost respect and reverence devoted toward the remains and the fallen soldier's family.

On the morning of 2 June 1968 I caught a supply truck from the Pink Palace for Dong Tam, a trip of about fifteen kilometers. Upon arriving there I found my way over to the Graves Registration Building. It was a two story wooden structure like hundreds of other buildings there. It was discreetly tucked away in an area not well traveled by passersby at the sprawling 9th Infantry Division Base Camp.

I found my way to the reception office located at one end of the building, introduced myself and presented my orders to a Staff Sergeant sitting behind a desk. He was not a particularly friendly fellow, as I recall, as he offered me to sit down. I was a Specialist Four (E-4) by then having been promoted from Private First Class in early April.

He shuffled through some papers on his desk in a matter of fact manner for about thirty seconds then stopped and looked up at me. He asked, "Do you know a soldier by the name of Corporal Daniel Lee Powell?" Still not getting it

I replied "Yeah sure, he's my best friend. He's up with a unit up north".

Without a moment's hesitation the Staff Sergeant said flatly "Corporal Powell was killed and you have been assigned to escort duty for his remains".

I sat there in shock for a minute before asking "When did this happen?" Looking down at papers on his desk he answered, "26 May, hostile action".

He had been dead for a week. For a moment I sat there dumbstruck. Then the Staff Sergeant looked at me, realizing my shock he said quietly, "You can take a few minutes if you like and come back in a half hour and we'll get your orders and paper work ready. You will need to hop a flight to Long Bien today. You will travel Priority One and you will be on a flight out of Bien Hoa for Travis Air Force Base in California tomorrow".

I went out of his office and walked around for a bit. With dirty, faded jungle fatigues I was wearing a bush hat, having left my steel pot at the Pink Palace. I was carrying the M-16 I got in trade from Pope for my M-60 machine gun a little more than twenty-four hours earlier. Infantrymen in Vietnam kept their weapons everywhere they went, twenty-four hours a day, checking them at the door only at service clubs on larger bases. Walking about I thought of the details of the past twenty-four hours and about how life had taken such a sudden and astonishing turn, I thought about Danny Powell and wondered how he had been killed.

I returned to the Graves Registration unit in a half hour and was seated in a folding chair next to a clerk typing out paperwork with instructions and orders I would need. The clerk was one of several sitting side by side on swivel office chairs at partitioned-off work stations, their backs to a walkway. He was a nice kid who was probably three or four years older than my nineteen, but he seemed like he was younger than me. All the clerks in the row were busy at their work stations, typing away and sharing office conversation about the paperwork of remains of the dead they were working through.

As I sat there the clerk sitting next to the guy processing Danny's papers looked up and absently said to no one in particular "how do you pronounce this guy's name...Etsitty, Etsitty"? Before any of the other clerks could respond I spoke up "that's Van Etsitty". He turned around looking at me in momentary disbelief. Then he asked how I knew. I told him that Etsitty was my assistant machine gunner.

He paused for a few seconds and asked, "Well did you know Oscar Phillips too? I think these two guys were in the same unit". I stared at him for a moment just thinking "Holy Crap, Oscar Phillips is dead too!"

I really thought Phillips was going to make it. Then I thought again about those bullet wounds in his lower abdomen and realized they had been much worse than I had allowed myself to believe. Oscar Phillips had survived for only one month and twenty-seven days of his one year tour of duty.

I told the clerk that Oscar Phillips was in my squad. He had been on an operation out in the Plain of Reeds. He looked at me for a minute and then he told he was sorry and then he asked me what the hell was happening out there?

These clerks processed the names of the dead everyday, but they almost never happened upon anyone who actually knew any of them. He said this was the busiest they had been since he had been working in Graves Registration and told me the 2nd of the 39th, our sister battalion had a very large number of KIA from the same area the day before. Thirty minutes later I walked out of Graves Registration with Danny Powell's file in a thick sturdy large envelope and four hundred dollars in travel cash, and headed for the air strip at Dong Tam to catch a shuttle flight for Long Bien.

I wondered how in the hell the Army had managed to locate me out in the Plain of Reeds and I wondered even more how I had been assigned this temporary duty that plucked me out of the middle of a war to travel half way around the world to bury my best friend. I was pretty much in shock with grief that I was too emotionally numb to sense.

Holding his file gave me a sense that I was doing something important for Danny, that I was his final keeper and sadly grateful to have the honor to be taking him back home and I wept dry tears of disbelief as I walked out of there.

31   Sad News on the Way Home

That afternoon I caught a twin engine Caribou on one of the shuttles that flew out of Dong Tam for Long Bien on the half hour during most daylight hours. They were cargo like rear ramp loaders that carried about twenty-four passengers plus pilots and crew. The Dong Tam airstrip was made of steel PSP and it seemed to be just barely long enough to accommodate the Caribou's takeoffs and landings. The passenger waiting area was a small wooden building with a counter at one end. Passengers flew on a first come first serve basis unless a soldier had priority one orders like mine that placed him at the top of the list for the next plane and in the front of every line in transit from Dong Tam to Oakland.

When I reported in at Long Bien I was processed right along with the regular military returnees that were heading for home upon completion of their Vietnam tours. I was given my flight departure time, assigned a billet for the night and issued new jungle boots, a khaki uniform with infantry brass, earned ribbons; Combat Infantry Badge and a Ninth Infantry Division patch to hang from my shirt pocket. I turned in my dirty boots and jungle fatigues and I was able to take my first hot shower since having left the states four months earlier.

I would depart on a chartered commercial passenger jet plane on the next day, 3 June, 1968. I was informed that Danny's remains were awaiting shipment at the military mortuary in Oakland. In those days there were no telephone calls made from Vietnam to the United States. Back in Southern California neither Danny's family nor mine knew that I was actually on the way.

It was strange to be granted the experience of returning home with the others. The mood of the returnees headed home was stark in contrast to my own. I knew that my time at home was to be short, that unlike the returnees, I was ordered to be back to this war following a very short sad visit back home. All the while I was still trying to mentally come to grips with the stunning and unexpected events of the previous forty-eight hours.

On 1 June I had somehow missed the Eagle Flight air assault that killed two of my squad members on the helicopter I would have flown. Two hours after that I was on my way to hot showers and a trip home.

When the TWA jet's landing gear left the runway at Bien Hoa Airbase on the morning of June 3rd the soldiers and airmen headed back to "the world" let out a long cheer with cries of so long and goodbye Vietnam. Vietnam was an alien universe to most of the troops serving there. It wasn't just a different time zone. It was on the other side of the International Dateline and the opposite side of the planet.

The long flight would require at least two refueling stops. Within the first two hours of the flight most passengers were napping. I talked with some of the guys on the flight telling them I was headed back on TDY, an acronym for temporary duty assignment. A few of them said that if they had had the chance to get out of Vietnam early they would never have gone back. That had begun to occupy my thinking too, but short of going to an army brig I could think of no other way of avoiding a return to infantry duty in the Mekong.

The first refueling stop was at Clark Air Force Base in the Philippines. We got off the plane to stretch our legs for a half hour in the terminal while the plane was re-supplied and refueled. As we were re-boarding the plane I heard some of the guys discussing some news they heard in the terminal.

Word was spreading that there had been an assassination attempt on Senator Robert Kennedy in Los Angeles. The senator, who was running for the Democratic nomination for President, was said to have been wounded. On transoceanic flights back then there was a news black out during the flight so there was no way of knowing any details of Kennedy's condition. We all remembered just five years earlier when President Kennedy was assassinated in Dallas and the murder of Martin Luther King just two months prior was still fresh in the minds of everyone too. The tenor of the mood was dimmed as we left the Philippines on the second leg of the flight but most were hopeful that Kennedy would be all right.

The flight took the polar route to Travis AFB in California. The second refueling stop was at Anchorage, Alaska. We had crossed the International Dateline during the long stretch from Clark AFB, having gone from day to night and back to daylight. What day it was no one cared. With each step closer to the U.S. the excitement grew. These were people who had been away for a year in an exotic country, many having endured dangerous combat and great hardship.

We touched down in Anchorage and entered the civilian terminal to stretch out. It was only then and there that we would learn that Senator Kennedy was dead. We watched news reports on a wall mounted TV at the airport during our brief layover and it was clear that the entire country seemed to be headed into shock and mourning over Senator Kennedy's death.

As we boarded the plane for the final leg to California there was a sense that the happy homecomings so many of these guys had been dreaming about for the past year would be dampened by the assassination of RFK. There was a sense that they had been cheated out of what would have been a special time by events that took precedent and were about to flood the consciousness of the Nation.

To me the assassination seemed to fit right in with the tragic chain of events that brought me from the Plain of Reeds three days before to be on this plane that would touch down in California within a couple of hours.

32 Riding on the Coast Starlight

After walking down the gangway to the tarmac at Travis Air Force Base some soldiers tossed Vietnamese money into the air and others literally kissed the tarmac after coming down the ladder from the plane. Homecomings from war are like that. Many of the men would be processed out of the Army within the next twenty-four hours, and those with time remaining to serve were headed home for thirty day leaves.

We were shown on to busses from Travis to the Oakland Army Base. Arriving at Oakland I was given VIP treatment. I felt like a full bird colonel. In all of my Army experience I was either getting yelled at or shot at. At Oakland I was introduced to an entirely different side of the military and it caught me off guard.

I was placed at the front of the line again and I traded in military payment certificates, the "funny money" used by the military in Vietnam, for U.S. greenbacks. After a shower and a meal I was fitted for a Class A uniform. Surprised to discover I had dropped nearly thirty pounds in my four months in Vietnam I cleaned up, dressed up and was out of there in four hours. Outside and free I took a taxi to a nearby hotel in town for which I had been given a voucher.

I walked into the hotel room and looked down at a bed with a mattress and clean sheets. The room had flush toilets, a bath and shower. In the bathroom I flushed the toilet just to watch it work. I had spent every night for months sleeping on the ground in the Mekong Delta. Four days and twelve thousand miles out of the Plain of Reeds I stood there watching the water swirl in the toilet bowl finding it difficult to get my mind wrapped around events.

I sat on the bed and placed a call home to Long Beach. Terry answered and I learned everything had been on hold there. They had been waiting for a call from me for days. They were told I was coming if I could be located, but there had been no guarantees. That was all they knew. We talked for awhile and I explained my orders were to report to the Oakland Army Base Mortuary the following morning to take responsibility for the remains and oversee the loading onto the Coast Starlight train's freight car.

The next morning we would take the train down the coast from Oakland to Los Angeles. In the early evening we would be met at the L.A. train depot by a representative from the civilian mortuary. I told Terry I'd call from the mortuary when I was finished there.

That night I shared a steak dinner at a nice restaurant in Oakland with a stateside based Air Force sergeant I met at the hotel where I was staying. He was a career guy, older than me, and he was on body escort duty too. It was a duty he had performed on a fairly regular basis. He didn't know the guy he was escorting. He bought dinner.

The following morning I took a taxi to the Oakland Army Base Mortuary where Danny Powell's remains awaited. It was an efficient operation. After signing some papers assigning their possession to me I headed for the train station. Within minutes of my arrival there a truck arrived and several military caskets were carefully loaded into a Coast Starlight freight car. Each casket had been assigned a military escort who stood in salute as his casket was placed into the freight car by forklift.

When Danny's casket appeared I did the same, only the reality of seeing his name on the box sent a shock and a chill through me. After all these months I was finally with him again and I could not help but feel that Danny was looking down upon me at that very instant, and I hoped he was happy to see that I was there and caring for him.

The casket itself was encased in a plywood shipping box painted battleship gray. CPL Daniel Lee Powell was stenciled in black at the foot of the box above his serial number. I stood in salute as it was placed into the door of the freight car thinking about Danny lying inside. Danny Powell, the ten year old kid who moved in next door. The kid who played the trumpet in the Gahr High School Band, who had a bit part in the high school play "Annie Get Your Gun" just a year earlier. Jesus Christ, I thought "neither of us would be here if you hadn't pulled that volunteer for the draft bullshit stunt just thirteen months ago".

The box with Danny was just one of seven military caskets bearing the U.S. Army's dead from Vietnam carried in that freight car from Oakland to Los Angeles on that single day.

I boarded the train and we headed south toward Los Angeles. Sitting in a passenger seat as the train made its way south I felt a kinship with him knowing Danny was on the train with me. I tried with little success to avoid thinking about how he might have been killed and wondering if he had suffered.

Robert F. Kennedy's death was consuming everyone. RFK had been running for President as a peace candidate to end the Vietnam War and some guy named Sirhan Sirhan shot him dead in a hotel kitchen in Los Angeles the day before. As I rode the train in my Class "A" U.S. Army uniform some people seemed to look on me as a symbol of something they hated. No one spoke to me and I couldn't figure out why I felt the hostility. They just glanced, and some stared.

On the long ride down the California coast my mind bounced between Danny Powell, Long Beach, my brother Terry and the wondering what was going on right now with Charlie Company back in Plain of Reeds,

When we finally arrived at the Los Angeles Train Depot it was early evening. I stood in salute again as they forklifted the box containing Danny's casket off the freight car and into the back of the windowless van the Patterson and Snively Mortuary had dispatched up to Los Angeles to pick up the remains and drive me down to the mortuary in Long Beach. When we arrived there I called home and spoke to my dad, informing him I was at the mortuary and ready to be picked up.

In fifteen minutes my mom and dad arrived and we all exchanged hugs. My mother was pretty shocked that I had lost so much weight during four months in Vietnam.

We all knew the mortician. Wilbur Snively was active in the North Long Beach Brethren Church leading the congregation in songs every Sunday. He emerged through a door from the back of the mortuary and greeted us all in the front waiting room. After a few minutes of small talk he asked me to call and drop by the mortuary the next day to take care of some paperwork. He was well versed in military funerals and procedures, having officiated over them many times.

We walked outside and got into the folk's six year old Chrysler Imperial, mom seated between dad and me in the front seat. We talked some about the Powell family and the Kennedy slaying, saying little or nothing about the war. As we rode home I gazed out the car window at familiar sites of life moving along in a seemingly normal fashion, all the more amazed to find myself in Long Beach, California on June 5th, 1968.

33　A Time for Funerals

Terry had just completed his second year of college at Long Beach City College. He was driving a White 1961 Mercury Comet, a dependable bomb of a car. When I arrived at the house ten minutes later he and I exchanged greetings and talked about the situation in the manner only twins can understand. We were told that when we were toddlers the two of us spoke in our own language and we had always kept an ability to communicate with our own inside jokes, nods and body language.

We headed out to our rooms out in the garage behind the house to talk. Terry explained to me how I had come to be ordered to escort Danny home. Some Army brass showed up at Larry and Ruth Powell's door around the 28th of May with an Army Chaplain. At first they told them that Danny was listed as missing in action, and that they had no further details. Then they returned the following day and informed them that their son, Corporal Daniel Lee Powell, had been killed in action. They had no details as to how he died.

At that moment, amidst questions about when Danny's body would be coming back and talk of burial services the Army would provide, and in the deepest throes of her grief Ruth Powell demanded to the Chaplain then and there that I was to be allowed to come home for his services.

They attempted to explain that only immediate family members serving in the military are granted bereavement leave, and the fact that I was serving in Vietnam would render this next to impossible.

Ruth Powell was not to be deterred. Terry explained how she called her United States Congressman's office and finally reached the Commanding General at Fort Mac Arthur in Los Angeles. Somehow strings got pulled and there I was.

My room out in the garage was just as I'd left it. I dumped my duffle bag there and Terry and I hopped in his Comet and headed over to the Powell's small rental house in Artesia. I had no civilian clothes that still fit so I wore the uniform. The folks would be along soon after us in the Chrysler.

When we arrived Ruth came out of the side door and met me in the driveway. She hugged me for at least two minutes, non-stop tears flowing down on to the shoulder of my uniform as Larry, sisters, Becky and Sharon surrounded us.

It was melancholy and joy. Ruth finally stepped away and with hands on my shoulders looked up upon me like I was a ghost returned from the dead. And in truth she was nearly right. The fact that I had been yanked out of Charlie Company in the middle of the campaign going on in the Plain of Reeds, on account of Danny's death and Ruth's relentless crusade to bring me home, was not lost on me.

Inside relatives and friends were gathered. Friends and neighbors the Powell's had never before met brought casseroles and desserts. Larry Powell sat quietly alone and Sharon, only nine years old, sampled the food assortment seemingly understanding little. Danny's sister, Becky, now just sixteen and in high school, was in a state of confused shock. Becky had been closer to Danny than anyone in his family and it was impossible for her to comprehend what the war was about and how her only brother was now dead at the age of nineteen.

The funeral was to be held on Saturday, the 8th of June. The Patterson and Snively Mortuary had been prepared to schedule the services for several days, depending on my arrival with the remains. The army had listed "non-viewable" on the paperwork and Ruth said they had decided on a closed casket. The funeral service would be held in the chapel of the North Long Beach Brethren Church. The Westminster

Memorial Park on Beach Boulevard off of the I-405 Freeway had graciously offered a free burial plot in the Park's Veterans section that was accepted.

I provided Larry and Ruth with the paperwork for the life insurance the army provided, showed them where to sign the claim and where to send it. They would receive $10,000 for the loss of their son, probably more money than either one had ever seen.

The next day I would stop at the mortuary for one more bit of paper signing. After that I was finished with the escort duty except for attending the funeral and gravesite service. When I was there Wilbur Snively quietly offered me an opportunity to view Danny's remains. Larry and Ruth had been there to see him and had given permission for me to view him. He said the military always listed remains as non-viewable, but that Danny was appropriate for viewing. He told me there only had only been a single, small entry wound on his chest. The offer was unexpected. I just thanked him and said I would prefer to remember Danny as I had known him.

The news hit Danny's high school. At a student assembly at Richard Gahr High School in Artesia, with the end of the 1968 school year and graduation just days away, the principal made the announcement: Danny Powell, a member of the 1967 graduating class, had been killed in action while serving with the United States Army in Vietnam the previous week, on May 26th.

Meanwhile all three of the television networks carried seemingly non-stop news stories that the body of slain United States Senator Robert F. Kennedy was lying in state inside St. Patrick's Cathedral in New York City. His body would be borne by funeral train on June 8th from New York to Washington, D.C. for burial at the Arlington National Cemetery.

When Saturday came I dressed in my Class "A" uniform and Terry drove us to the Chapel of the North Long

Beach Brethren Church for the funeral service. It was overflowing with friends, family and Danny's fellow students from Gahr High School. Terry had to be dragged to the service. He hated death and funerals, but he relented and sat alone in the back of the Chapel. I was seated in the front row next to Becky Powell. My parents were also up front with the Powell's.

The sight of the casket covered in the American Flag in the front of the chapel brought a flood of emotions I found hard to contain. Everyone around was shedding tears, and even though I was churning inside with emotions, to my surprise I found it was impossible to cry. I had become hardened by my training and combat and death. I knew I would shortly return to the war and my own survival instincts refused to free me. I sat through the service staring straight ahead, my heart beating fast, feeling numb.

It was a warm, sunny day. Following the Chapel Service I rode in the limousine with the family at their request from the chapel to the cemetery. I realized that to the Powell's I was family. I was Danny's brother. I felt truly honored to be there with them. I sat in the front, shotgun seat with a sad and bewildered sixteen year old Becky Powell seated next to me in the middle. There was a police escort from the Chapel to Westminster Memorial Park, and I counted more than fifty cars following the procession to the cemetery.

At the gravesite while family and friends watched and wept, a military honor guard carried the casket from the hearse to the grave, folded the flag from the casket and presented it to Ruth Powell on behalf of a grateful nation. There was a twenty-one gun salute and a bugler, stationed back and away from the gathering, played taps.

It was funeral all over the country. The only thing on television that day was coverage of the train bearing the body of Senator Kennedy from New York to Washington. When Danny's graveside service was over I thought about the hundreds of other soldiers, marines, sailors and airmen all over the country who were being buried the same way that week and every week throughout the country.

34   Time Back in the U.S.A.

My orders were to report to the Oakland Army Base seventy-two hours after the burial services to process back to Vietnam. I called Fort Mac Arthur and after explaining the situation I was authorized an additional five days of compassionate leave.

During the extra days Terry, our neighbor Joe Bradford and I hung out with friends. We met Joe when we moved to Long Beach in eleventh grade. The Bradford's lived two doors up from us on 63rd Street. He was Danny's age, a year in back of Terry and me at Jordan High School. The four of us had spent countless hours shooting hoops in the alley behind Joe's house on the basketball hoop mounted above the Bradford's garage door. Dennis Cable, my best friend since sixth grade in Paramount hung out with us too.

Terry and I both had fake ID cards that we had obtained the previous year by appearing at the DMV office in Bellflower by claiming to be our older brothers who had lost their driver's licenses. We filled out the paperwork in their names, paid the three dollars, had our pictures taken and a month later our brother's new licenses, with our pictures arrived by mail. Terry was Richard and I was Dennis. Things were simpler then.

We all hung out a lot in the garage that week talking things over, throwing down beers and even shooting some hoops behind Joe's garage. Terry and I also spent some time together shooting eight ball pool at the "Why Not?" on Cherry Avenue, a beer bar around the corner and a block south of our house.

A couple of days before I left for Vietnam I visited once again with the Powell's to say goodbye. Before I left Ruth shared some news. She'd just received a letter from a very distraught George Vander Dussen. In his letter George expressed anger and frustration with the way they were operating in the 198th Light Infantry Brigade.

It was the same story. They occupied ground and gave it right back. George told how Danny had died. They were camped on a hilltop. It was the very same hilltop they had occupied a couple of weeks before and left. When they came back the North Vietnamese Army had left booby traps for them. Danny set one off. He set his backpack and gear down for a chow break. Lifting the backpack after finishing his C-Rations triggered a grenade placed at eye level in a tree. The explosion's concussion knocked him unconscious to the ground. He was killed instantly and never knew what hit him. Two other soldiers were also seriously injured by the blast.

I was grateful to know how it happened and thankful to know he had not suffered. I shared goodbyes and hugs with Larry, Becky and Sharon Powell. Then I thanked Ruth once more, kissed her on the cheek, hugged her and left.

Two days later I caught the train north for the Oakland Army Base. Using my fake ID to buy drinks in the Coast Starlight's bar car I rode the train north and wracked my brain about what was going to happen when I arrived back at Charlie Company.

I wondered who and how many of my fellow soldiers in Charlie Company I might find injured or dead when I returned. I was afraid to find out. I knew one thing for certain: When I returned I would be a far different soldier than the one who flew out of the Plain of Reeds on June 1st.

By this time I knew the drill at the Oakland Army Base. Arriving there again I turned in my Class "A" dress greens for a khaki uniform for the flight back to Vietnam. That afternoon I was bussed to Travis AFB along with another group of unsuspecting new guys headed for Vietnam. At Travis my passenger status was priority standby, meaning I would wait for my name to be called to be added to the next flight out with room for standby passengers.

When my name was not called for the very first flight I took it as a sign from God. I stood up, walked out of the terminal, and headed for the bus waiting area where I casually boarded a bus headed back to the Oakland Army base. Wearing a uniform I didn't need a ticket. On the ride back to Oakland I decided I needed a personal vacation to think things out and I was not ready to head back to Vietnam just yet. It was precisely at this point in my US Army career that I became something of an independent operator.

I had a standing invitation to stay at Uncle Bill and Aunt Dorothy's house up in San Rafael. When I got to Oakland I gave Dorothy a call. "Come on up and stay as long as you like", she told me and Uncle Bill, who had spent WW II in the US Navy, drove down to pick me up an hour later. Having traveled half way around the world it seemed a shame to head right back. The army had given me an extra week in the states so I decided to take another on my own.

One of the curious things I noticed during my time in California those few days was everywhere I went, whether riding in a vehicle or walking down a sidewalk I was constantly surveying to my left and right and I always knew, wherever I was, exactly where I would dive for cover in the event automatic weapons were to open up. I knew it was not going to happen but I could not keep myself from doing this. I was conditioned to it.

I spent the week at Bill and Dorothy's house hanging out in civilian clothes. I took in a couple of movies with Uncle Bill and had a night out at Zach's Bar and Grill in Sausalito with my cousin Billy and his girlfriend watching the turtle races, drinking and dancing. Uncle Bill put me up in a room at the end of his house with its own liquor bar, a view of the San Rafael Bridge and ten years worth of issues of Playboy magazines.

Finally after six days I asked Uncle Bill to give me a ride to Oakland. Reluctantly, I faced the fact that I would never be able to live with myself if I ran off to Canada or refused to return to Vietnam. The bottom line was I now had brothers in arms still getting shot at, and in spite of the futility I felt about the war I had a responsibility to go back.

I put on my uniform and got ready to go. Uncle Bill drove me to the Oakland Army Base where I caught a shuttle bus to Travis. Inside the terminal I reported my name at the counter. The airman there gawked at me, shook his head and asked where I had been. They had been calling my name for every flight for a week. I told him I just decided to take a few days off. Looking up at me he smiled, and said "I don't blame you". A half hour later I was belted into a big jet airliner headed back to Vietnam.

35 Back to Tan Tru

On the flight back it occurred to me that this was going to be my second tour. In four and one-half months I had come full circle. Off to war and back. I was now going back again. We flew back with a refueling stop at Yokoda, Japan then down to Bien Hoa in Vietnam. We were bussed to Long Bien where I traded in my khakis for newly minted jungle fatigues.

Everyone at Long Bien thought I was a new arrival just as I has been in February. But it was now nearly July and I had seven plus months remaining on my tour. I had my own set of orders so I did not have to go through the drill again at the 90th Replacement Battalion. Right off I found my way to the Post Exchange and purchased Spec. Four collar badges and a Combat Infantryman Badge (CIB) for my brand new jungle fatigue shirt. I did not want to be confused with the new replacements I arrived with.

I went to the Enlisted Men's Club there, ordered a beer and sat down at a table with a bunch of the new arrivals, the only men in there. A couple of the new guys there looked at my CIB and accused me of wearing something I had not yet earned. I looked for all purposes just like the rest of them. I explained my situation. They didn't believe me, but I didn't care what they believed.

I decided to take my sweet time returning to Charlie Company, still apprehensive about what I would find there, like who had been killed while I had been gone. And I was in no hurry to return to the field.

A day later I caught a Caribou to Dong Tam. When I got there I went to the EM Club. There I ran into a couple of guys who told me that the 2nd of the 60th had left the Pink Palace and was back at Tan Tru. I was glad to hear this. I figured out that the battalion brass had little or no idea that I was back in country so I decided I would stay in Dong Tam for a few days and milk the situation before returning.

I needed a place to stay and I figured out that I could wander around and hang out at any of a dozen or so units, grabbing meals and a bunk to sleep in without anyone asking who the heck I was or really caring. I found out that a Catholic Chaplain there had a safe house where any soldier could grab a bunk and hang out with no questions asked.

When I went there one night with a black guy I met at the Dong Tam EM Club for the first time I was pretty drunk. We walked in and found a dozen guys there smoking grass and listening to Jimi Hendrix under a black light with psychedelic posters. It was pretty neat. I stayed there for about three nights, spending days at the Dong Tam Recreation Center where electric guitars could be checked out and pool tables were available.

I met a guy there who was doing much the same as me. He played a mean Fender Telecaster. He told me he was a guitar player for the Swinging Medallions before he got drafted, a band that had a hit record..."Double Shot of My Baby's Love", a song I remembered and liked.

I came across a staff sergeant there at Dong Tam newly arrived at division. He was checking out an M-16 at division supply and I was struck by his appearance. He was a man in his thirties and I sized him up as a guy who had been out of the Army and had re-enlisted for the express purpose of coming to Vietnam, He was about five foot seven with an athletic build, short graying buzz cut hair, strike fatigues with a Ranger rope tied on his chest and a Ranger patch on his shoulder. I remember thinking this guy was a gung ho trooper and I hoped he was not headed for Tan Tru. I didn't give it much thought until we struck up a short conversation when he told me he was headed for the 2nd of the 60th and on his way to Tan Tru. His name was Leo Mons.

I spent a week at Dong Tam before I decided it was time to face the music and head back to Tan Tru. In the morning I caught a re-supply truck out of Dong Tam for Tan Tru. I couldn't believe I was really going back to Charlie Company but I had run out of options.

When I got to there I walked into the Orderly Room and checked in. On the wall behind the company clerk was a white board of sorts with personnel statuses in grease pencil. At the top of the board I saw my name under the status labeled A.W.O.L. (Absent without Leave). First Sergeant Francis Bobo was still there, and he was called out from his room at the back of the OR to see to me. "Where the hell have you been, Brooks?" he barked out at me. Looking up at the board I replied calmly, "Well, I've been A.W.O.L. Top".

He was befuddled by my candor. He told me to get over to supply and get my gear. I said "OK, but I'm not going out to the field anymore". He said, "And why do you say that?" I had not rehearsed this moment at all, and I really didn't know what I was going to do or say then, but I replied to him straight up, "Because I don't see any future in it Top". And then I told him that you cannot send a man back to the world to bury his brother with full military honors, watch his mother and family cry and then bring him back and casually expect him to hump the paddies in this shit again like nothing happened.

It was immediately apparent First Sergeant Bobo did not give a shit. First Sergeant Bobo was a six foot five inch career First Sergeant who was the spitting image of Fess Parker. When he first came to Charlie Company shortly before I did, he had insisted on going out on operations with the company. He carried an outdated M-14 rifle which he insisted on, an outdated weapon that weighed much too much to hump out in the Mekong Delta mud and canals. After a few more firefights using the M-14, including the April 17th event, the company commander told him his job was to stay in base camp.

He was not one to be messed with. But I think he must have had some idea of who I was, and where I had just been. He let the moment slide. The company was in the field that afternoon and I guess he needed time to figure out how to deal with me. After he dismissed me I wandered back to my old third platoon hooch.

Everything looked different. I found a vacant bunk. I went to supply, checked out an M-16 and combat gear and went back and made myself a place on a bunk.

When the guys came in that afternoon the ones I recognized were amazed that I had returned. I had been away for more than three weeks. Ron Cavett was still there and he filled me in on recent events.

During my absence it seemed everything changed in Charlie Company. Sergeant Holloway was taken off the line, having received his third or fourth Purple Heart. Doc Sherrf, our platoon medic, was gone, wounded by a gunshot in a firefight. He was thought to be in a hospital at Cam Ranh Bay. Our friend Bill Sommers over in the first platoon was medevaced out to a military hospital too, having earned his second Purple Heart upon being badly wounded by shrapnel from a grenade tossed at him by a VC while out on night ambush.

Sergeant Ed Ryan had taken an AK 47 round through the side of his neck from a distance of two feet from a VC in a bunker they had assaulted on June 8th. The round exited his back by his shoulder blade. It had not hit anything vital and he was going to be okay. When he was shot, Ed Crane had pulled him unconscious from a wet paddy and carried him to a dust off and had saved his life. Ryan had been awarded the Silver Star for valor for his actions that day in addition to his second Purple Heart and Crane was awarded a Bronze Star for valor for the action, and he was taken off the line too.

Tom Edmond, the Captain's RTO (radio operator) who came through the third platoon was killed on the same day Ryan was shot, and Sgt. Charles Huzico, the guy who proudly carried the name of his home town of Struthers, Ohio inked in large dark letters on the side of his camouflaged helmet cover, had died from gunshot wounds just a couple days before, on June 25th.

So there we were. Ron Cavett and I were left. And the heart of our squad leadership in the third platoon was gone within less than a month's time. Wayne Pope was still there carrying the M-60 I had given to him on June 1st and a bunch of the April arrivals were now becoming seasoned warriors. Sergeant Clark was getting wigged out on a regular basis and wanted out of the game. Our CO, Captain Cadigan had been shot in the foot and was on crutches but he was still the CO, only riding up in the C&C chopper with the Lieutenant Colonel trying to direct operations from the sky.

First Sergeant Bobo and the brass had no idea how to deal with me. I didn't give them any ideas either. I walked around during the days acting like a crazy man playing with a yoyo, and I pulled perimeter bunker guard duty at night. I carried on like this for almost a week. Meanwhile Ron Cavett, who by some miracle had yet to get scratched, was getting more and more pissed about everything.

I was becoming something of a celebrity in the company with a lot of the men. They could not figure out how I managed to get this scam over on the CO and the First Sergeant. And as it turned out I really didn't.

It all abruptly ended one evening when the third platoon was set to head out on an ambush patrol a couple of klicks down Tan Tru Road. Just before the platoon headed out I was summoned into the Orderly Room and surrounded by two Lieutenants, the First Sergeant, and a JAG Officer I did not recognize. He held in one hand an open copy of the Uniform Code of Military Justice and read from it. In front of the assembled brass and NCO's he gave me a "lawful order" to return to the field and join my platoon on the patrol.

I paused for a few seconds, looked around at the assembled witnesses, and then I said simply, "Okay".

They had set me up and I knew they had me. I walked down the steps from the orderly room, into the platoon hooch, grabbed my M-16, put a dozen magazines in my various pockets, grabbed a canteen and insect repellant, put on my newly issued helmet liner and steel pot headgear and joined my platoon mates. I was back on the line, back in the field.

36   A Reluctant Warrior

I had no illusions that surviving Vietnam was pretty much a crap shoot, but I had decided that I would do my best to help make that happen. I knew that spending less time one spent out in the field, making air assaults increased ones odds of survival, and I also knew that there were small but not insignificant actions one could take out in the field that also helped.

One of the first things I did when I returned to the field was to take a knee whenever possible. By this I meant when the company or platoon was moving through the delta there were many times when the line of men, spread out in a line moving forward would come to a complete stop while the point man stopped to survey the ground ahead, or perhaps look for a crossing point over a canal. I had learned through experience that these were the times when the enemy troops were most likely to open fire on us. So I began to take a knee every time we stopped.

When I first did this the men around me looked at me as if I was nuts. So I explained my reasons, including my whole survival odds theory. I told them that if I were a Viet Cong bunkered at the edge of the wood line getting ready to fire on Americans I would pick out the best targets. And the guy(s) kneeling down were not the best targets. At first the others thought I was being excessively cautious, until a half hour later we were stopped again and the VC opened up on us.

The men around me all came diving behind the paddy dike only to find me already there. The next time we stopped, my entire squad took a knee. And after a few days, most of the company began to routinely take a knee near a dike for cover whenever we were stopped on patrol. I was motivated not just by my wish for survival. It was also a belief that the whole fucking war was a waste if it was going to be fought in the manner the military chose to fight it.

We went out on another Bushmaster a few days later and had set up undetected in a wood line for the night. The VC had no idea we were there. That night I was looking across a rice paddy through a Starlight Scope. The paddy was dry and the next wood line was about 200 meters away. At about ten PM I watched as an entire company of Viet Cong walked along the edge of the wood line. They had their weapons slung on their shoulders brazenly smoking cigarettes and using flashlights to light their way along. Through the Starlight Scope I counted 118 of them heading in the direction of a wood line with a small village to our left.

There was no way we would fire on them with just 60 of us lying prone without much cover in our wood line, but we had a direct bead on where they were. So we whispered on the radio to bring artillery fire on them. The response we got was that they were in an area where there were "friendlies", and the fire mission was not approved. Instead Battalion directed us to quietly move a platoon across the open paddy diagonally in their direction.

The third platoon was elected. So a squad of twelve of us crossed out into the paddy in the night darkness. When we came within 100 meters of the wood line we stopped behind a dike and waited. We were instructed to fire a few rounds their way to see if they would return fire. Twelve of us lying behind that dike came to a collective conclusion…yeah, right. We had enough sense to ignore this stupid order.

This was but one more example for me that the grunt on the ground was nothing more than a replaceable part in the war plan. Never mind pounding these brazen jackasses smoking cigarettes and using flashlights, as they strolled through the night, with artillery. Just send a platoon out to take some pot shots at them. I had never seen so many VC in one place totally ripe for the taking.

Sixty was always the magic number. It was the number needed to fill the ten slicks for air assaults for Eagle Flights. Six men from Charlie Company were killed during the first twenty five days in June alone. You didn't have to be a mathematician to calculate that if you were one of the sixty men going out every day for twelve months of your tour, the odds of getting killed were pretty strong. The brass understood this too. That's why most grunts in our unit were allowed to be taken off the line after surviving about eight or nine months.

With seven months left in Vietnam I figured I had to stay alive for at least another three months in order to maybe get off the line. In the 2nd of the 60th they rarely brought in people with a clerk or supply MOS. They just filled those kinds of slots with 11 Bravos who had spent their time on the line. My goal was to become one of these.

I was back in the field but I had not given up my quest for survival. In early August the company clerk wandered around asking if anyone wanted to use one of the R&R (rest and recreation) leaves that had been allocated to Charlie Company. During your tour of duty every soldier was given a five day R&R plus one seven day leave. On R&R or leave you went into Camp Alpha in Saigon and were given a free air transport to any one of several cities throughout Asia or even Hawaii or Australia. I spoke right up. There was even another allocated R&R that no one was taking.

Our field strength was so low that we didn't even have enough people who were available to take our allocated R&R slots. I figured the number of R&R slots coming down from division was probably based on a presumption that every company had at least 100 men. But in April Charlie Company's field strength had been down to less that 50 men, and it was only about 70 now. In most cases you became eligible for an R&R leave after about six months in country. I was close enough. My R&R was approved and in August I was headed for Camp Alpha in Saigon. An R&R could get you 12 days off the line if you milked your time getting back, twelve days closer to the golden day when you might get off the line. I milked it for every day I could.

Geoffrey Kerber, a guy from Palo Alto, California was relatively new to the company at the time. Even though he had been in country for just a couple months I urged him to take one of the R&R slots. One of the secrets I had learned by then was nobody really kept close tabs on the number of R&Rs one took. They were too busy to keep track. If you could get an R&R in month two you could probably take another one in month six or seven. So Kerber, after thinking it over for about two minutes, spoke up to take it, and to his surprise they approved it. The next week Kerber and I went off to Hong Kong together.

After I returned to the line I found that a lot of the new guys were looking to me for advice. It seemed I'd developed a reputation that I could help them put the situation into the proper perspective. So I told any one of the recent arrivals who would listen that they had but one goal over there, to make it back home. We all had our duties to perform but this was no place to try to be a hero. It was the same kind of advice I had been given from men like Ed Ryan, Ed Crane and John Cleary when I first arrived. It helped me a lot and I felt I had the same responsibility to help these guys.

It took some time to figure out the tactics employed in the Delta were geared toward drawing out the enemy by using infantrymen as bait. Swooping out of the sky right down in front of bunker lined wood lines in a row of Hueys was a pretty effective way to get the VC shooting away. So commanders flying high above and out of danger could say,"Oh yes! I just knew the little bastards were down there"! And if some poor young Spec Four, PFC or 2nd

Lieutenant with four months in country died in the process, well that was just war. Shit happens and sometimes men die.

Aside from the fact that nothing was ever achieved in the long run, the VC always came back and we always went back to Tan Tru or the Pink Palace or wherever the battalion was holed up at the time, the tactics of dumping choppers full of grunts right on top of the bad guys was completely unnecessary. There were lots of other ways that the enemy could have been located and dispatched without getting so many people killed. But helicopter assault tactics in the Mekong Delta were the established dogma. That was just the way it was done and nothing was going to change it. At least not in this war.

So most of us who lived long enough finally figured it out. There was really no end game there except for each individual combatant to get through his tour alive. The brass (officers with the rank of Major and above) rarely got killed, but they got their tickets punched for future promotions on the backs of the guys out humping the paddies.

As it would turn out it would take a lot longer than three more months before I would get off the line. By this time I was not popular with some of the battalion higher-ups, many of whom loved hard charging new troops fresh in from the States. Fact of the matter was the longer one survived his combat tour over there the more careful one became. The last thing they wanted was some kid like me taking the fire out of the new blood.

37 Busted

In late August I was summoned to Major Bernard Loeffke's private, bunkered home/office that was located near the main headquarters building at Tan Tru. Major Loeffke was the battalion's executive officer (XO). He was a West Point graduate and a very strike dresser. His fatigues were always stateside quality starched and his jungle boots always shined. He never spent a day in the field that I ever knew of except for manning the C&C chopper high in the sky a time or two when Lieutenant Colonel John Lindsay, the battalion CO, was away.

In his book about his tour commanding the 9th Division's fourth of the thirty-ninth infantry battalion the year after I left Vietnam, the late Colonel David Hackworth had some choice words for Loeffke, who apparently stayed on in Vietnam punching his ticket on his way to eventually becoming a Major General, before retiring from the US Army. According to Colonel Hackworth Loeffke later became the guy at the 9th Infantry Division who approved the medals awarded to the division's brass.

On this particular day I was told to stay back at Tan Tru while the company went out. So I was spending the day taking my turn at guarding a young black PFC by the name of Farrell from the battalion, awaiting military justice, who was arrested in Saigon allegedly working the black market for six months. I sat there that day chatting with him sipping on a cold beer, armed with a forty-five holstered on my hip while he filled sand bags, when I was called in to Loeffke's private compound. Loeffke's aid-de-camp took out a comb and cleaned up my hair before I entered his sand bagged, bunkered sanctum.

It was like a visit to the school principal. Major Loeffke had me sit down across from him at his desk. He congratulated me on my good work having returned to field duty, and he told me I was a fine looking young soldier. Then he told me he was giving me an Article 15, punishment short of a court marshal, for my having been AWOL on my way back from body escort duty in California. I was cited for six days AWOL, busted from Spec Four down to PFC and fined sixty dollars.

I signed the Article 15, thanked the man and left. I didn't like the sixty dollar fine but at the time I didn't really give a crap about the rank. Most guys in the field didn't wear any rank on their fatigues anyway and it made no difference as to my duties.

I guess it must have been my week to be called in on the carpet. A couple days after I was busted by Major Loeffke we arrived back at Tan Tru in the afternoon following the day's operation. I was told the battalion chaplain wanted to speak to me about a matter of some importance. The battalion chaplain held the rank of Captain. Captain Thomas Hines was a quiet, well respected Protestant of some kind. I had never previously spoken with him nor had I ever attended any religious services he officiated. I had seen and heard him pray at a memorial service or two held at battalion, but that was the extent of my knowledge of the man.

I walked over to his small chapel located near the headquarters building and knocked on his door. We exchanged pleasantries with no salutes and he offered me a chair next to his desk. He held in his hand a letter addressed to him as battalion chaplain from my mother. In the letter my mother asked the chaplain to admonish me for not writing her. Upon hearing his words telling me this I was pretty much speechless.

When I first arrived in Vietnam I sent a letter home to my mother each and every week. In fact we were instructed by our commanders to do so. In my first four months in Vietnam, prior to the body escort trip home, my mother had written me a grand total of one letter. When I arrived back in country I wrote to her a couple of times when I first returned, and hearing no response I had written to her no more. So here I was, in the seventh month of my tour, having received but one single letter from my dear beloved mother, sitting in the battalion chaplain's office while he read to me from a letter from her complaining that her soldier son has neglected to write her.

I told this to Captain Hines and added, "This pretty much sums up my mother". I thanked him and left his office but before leaving I asked him to write and tell my dear mother that I would gladly write to her, a promise I promptly kept a month later.

38 Letters

A lot of the guys that came in with the April wave of replacements were first class soldiers. Wayne Pope was doing a great job carrying the M-60 and it was his to keep as far as I was concerned. A kid named Scofield from West Virginia or South Carolina or some state thereabouts, and another lanky Southern kid named Spalding became the regular point men for the platoon. Geoff Kerber was a natural leader and destined to becoming a squad leader in the not too distant future. And amazingly, we still had a couple of the original guys from October around. One of them, Joe Johnson, a black guy from Atlanta never missed a day in the field and was one of the very few men I knew of that would stay on the line in Charlie Company's third platoon for his entire tour. But by and large the October guys would be mostly gone or off the line by August.

I would never quite fit in with the platoon like I had before June. I kept a low profile most of the time, hoping mostly in vain that the company leadership would forget about me. One big difference by mid July was the Army was obviously running short of career noncommissioned officers and junior field officers too. Lieutenants in the field never lasted long. Even if they had only six months of field duty most of ours ended up wounded or dead.

My brother, Terry wrote to me on a regular basis to keep me up on things back at the home front, and I made it a point to write him as often as I could. In July I also penned a letter to George Vander Dussen, still up north with the 198th L.I.B. I told George about Danny's service and asked him to write when he had time with any details about Danny's experience there.

Mail Call was a big deal in Vietnam. In the days before the internet or even routine intercontinental telephone service letters from home mail call was the only lifeline to the "world". I rarely ever got any mail and I had long since stopped showing up for mail call. When I did get a letter someone would find me and bring it around.

On a day in late July they brought me a letter. It was returned mail. It was the very letter I had written to Danny Powell back in April. It had a half dozen red ink stamped words on both sides. "RETURN TO SENDER" and "DECEASED" were stamped all over it. I had sent it three weeks before Danny was killed but it never reached him, and it had taken several weeks to find its way back to me at Tan Tru.

At Tan Tru after the day's operation a couple of weeks later I got another letter. This one was from Ruth Powell. Ruth had stayed in touch with George Vander Dussen's mom after Danny was killed. I had been looking for a letter from George for several weeks.

When I opened the letter I got a bad feeling. Ruth told me she had received some news from George's mom. She wrote that George had been riding in a three quarter ton truck when a grenade hanging from the dashboard somehow fell from its glove box handle. The cotter pin came out and the grenade detonated inside the cab of the truck. The accident happened on the Fourth of July. George was critically injured.

He died in a military hospital in Vietnam six days later, on July 10th. I stared at the letter in disbelief. My mind went back to our New Year's Eve drinking fest with my twin brother Terry, Danny, George and me at George's house in Artesia when we were on leave just seven months ago. I thought back to the afternoon outside the barracks at Fort Ord in basic training when I first met George. And I thought about George's young wife and his twin sister.

I thought again about Danny Powell and Bobby Kennedy's funeral train and the funerals for countless young soldiers back home taking place every day, and the politicians trying to figure out how to get re-elected. It all made no sense.

The country back home seemed to be breaking apart when we were jumping off choppers and hitting the paddies. Danny was dead and George was dead and Oscar Phillips was dead and Van Etsitty was dead and Charlie Huzico was dead and Edmond was dead and Bill Sommers was in the hospital and Holloway and Ed Ryan and Doc Sherrf were wounded and gone off the line.

And I was totally fucked just sitting there on a canvas cot in the third platoon hooch at Tan Tru staring at that letter.

38 Jitterbugging with Shake and Bake Staff Sergeants

When August finally rolled around it was difficult to find a single man in Charlie Company with a rank above E-6 who went out to the field on company sized operations, including Eagle Flights. Staff Sergeant Mons was running the third platoon and despite the early apprehensions about him because of his Ranger dress and buzz cut, he quickly earned the respect and admiration of his men. He was smart and his allegiances rested with the PFCs, Spec 4s and young buck sergeant draftees who were humping the paddies and taking fire every day. The company commander was on crutches and we were out of lieutenant platoon leaders. For awhile the only officer who hit the field with Charlie Company was the company's artillery forward observer.

The NCO situation was dire. To try to deal with the NCO problem the Ninth Infantry Division established an NCO Training Academy at Dong Tam called the Reliable Academy, where promising young Spec Fours and buck sergeants could attend an in-country training program for a few weeks and emerge as what were called Instant NCO's. The Instant NCO's were then returned to their units with the rank of staff sergeant and assigned as squad leaders and platoon sergeants.

Meanwhile Colonel Hank "Gunfighter" Emerson, running the Ninth Infantry Division's First Brigade's Recondo Brigade was perfecting his "jitterbug" helicopter assault tactics and making one hell of a name dumping grunts on top of VC bunker protected wood lines and racking up phantom body counts some idiot ordered to be posted on the wall of the battalion mess hall like a scoreboard. And my buddy Ron Cavett, from Pawnee, Oklahoma was still pretty much pissed off about just about everything.

All the while another kid named Vedmore had somehow perfected the art of assuming a permanent position as the keeper of Tan Tru's Bunker 16 on the perimeter next to Charlie Company. Vedmore was a stocky guy from Connecticut who arrived in April and he had managed to get himself a permanent position manning the tripod mounted M-60 machine gun on Bunker 16. He never was called to hit the chopper pad. That M-60 there was Vedmore's baby. He spent 24 hours a day on that bunker and never left it except to take a crap. I loved the guy.

In August we added an Instant NCO who had gone into the NCO Academy an E-4 and came out an E-6, and was soon assigned as a platoon Sergeant in Charlie Company. At the end of August we found ourselves on a company sized operation following the third or fourth helicopter assault of the day without a single line officer left on the ground. The CO was still hobbled and on crutches and was flying up above the action in the battalion's command and control (C&C chopper).

It was August 30th and the Huey helicopter assault company that was providing our air assets that day was scheduled for other duties come 1700 hours. As we plodded in toward a wood line enclosed open paddy we were notified we had less than thirty minutes to call the slicks back out to extract the company.

Undeterred, the young hero Instant NCO convinced the CO riding above to allow the company to patrol just one more rice paddy deeper into the interior before pulling us out. He was leading a full infantry company on the ground all by himself for the first time and I guess he was determined to make the most of it. As a member of the company that day I can assure you I was not inspired, and neither was anyone else out there that afternoon.

As we approached the interior rice paddy opening we noted a swimming pool sized B-52 bomb crater in the center of the paddy. The water table filled it from the bottom leaving about three feet dry from ground level. But as we approached into the wood line on the right side of the interior paddy machine gun fire rang out from inside the wood line. But for some reason it was firing in the opposite direction away from our position. Most of us thought our point man, already inside the wood line, was the person doing the firing until he came running out telling us that it was a VC who was doing the shooting.

We took cover behind a dike on the edge of the opening as the machine gun rotated its fire in a half circle until it was firing at us. It soon became apparent the VC deep inside the wood line could hear us but couldn't figure out at first from what direction we were approaching.

He was firing from a mounted AK-50 machine gun and he soon swung the barrel around to our direction. Our platoon was pinned behind the dike closest to the clearing with the B 52 crater about fifteen meters in front of us. Charlie Company's First Platoon was pinned behind another dike about thirty meters behind us precluding them from returning fire toward the mounted AK 50 without hitting us. Bottom line was we couldn't move and the AK 50 was only 15 or 20 meters away and it had a bead on us.

I don't know who the hero was that day. It might have been our Instant NCO, but somebody crawled up to the bunker holding the VC with the machine gun and tossed a fragmentation grenade in it. When it blew we could feel the ground shake and the muffled sound a grenade makes when it blows a VC bunker. Following the explosion the hero came walking out of the wood line carrying the VC's AK machine gun.

A couple minutes later we got an "all clear" and were ordered up. We began moving out across the open paddy next toward the wood line where the VC had been. We wanted to cross to the forward paddy dike ahead on the other side of the B 52 crater, and move into a larger open paddy on the other side where we could bring in slicks to take us out of there and back to Tango Tango (Tan Tru).

When the third platoon reached the halfway point to the dike ahead at least three AK's opened up on us on full automatic from the same wood line where the AK 50 bunker had been blown. We were completely exposed in the open paddy and fire was coming at us from no more than 15 meters away.

Most of us retreated back to the cover behind the dike we had just left and two of three guys jumped down into the B 52 crater. As we reached the safety of the dike with a dive some of us were actually feeling our own bodies for bullet wounds, incredulous that we had not been hit. It was apparent that the original shooter had not been alone, and there were at least three more VC alive and bunkered inside the wood line.

The next hour and a half was difficult. We were pinned down and any movement we made was met with automatic weapons fire. The First Platoon was still stuck behind us and we no longer had air assets. It looked as if we might be stuck out there all night.

I found I could lift my head above the dike for maybe three seconds to reconnoiter before ducking back down to avoid getting a bullet. One of the men pinned down and stuck in the B 52 crater pool was Wayne Pope with his M-60 machine gun. Another guy out there was a young PFC who had been ordered to tote a squawk box case with a bull horn on his back. Inside was a battery powered megaphone some idiot thought our Vietnamese Tiger Scout could use to talk to some VC into surrendering should the opportunity arise. There were three new bullet holes through the case but the PFC was okay.

Over the next hour our young hero took charge and crawled into the jungle and amazingly, he was able to blow two more bunkers and come out with the enemy weapons each time. I sure as hell hated that he had volunteered us into this situation but had to admit the guy had guts.

About ten minutes after he had blown the last bunker two VC went tearing across the paddy just behind the dike on the other side of the B 52 crater. Someone yelled "there they go!" and every guy in the Third Platoon opened up on them at once. It was like a shooting gallery and they both went down.

It seemed like it might be safe to finally move out but first someone had called for a dust off behind us. The helicopter landed within about ten minutes setting down in a clearing on the back side of the First Platoon's position behind us. They brought a stretcher and a body bag. Danny Bittner, 21 a young Spec Four from Virginia had been hit with an AK-47 round in the neck when we were pinned down.

Two nights earlier Bittner and I had shared beers and conversation for a couple hours at the Tan Tru Enlisted Men's Club. It was the first time I had any time to get to know him and he was a hell of a good guy. I had the sinking feeling that he might well have been shot, situated as he was behind our position, by a VC shooting at me when I had been poking my head up and ducking back down to reconnoiter. I will never know. Danny Bittner had survived five and a half months of his one year tour of duty.

After they took his body out we finally got up and moved out once again over the paddy where we had been ambushed 90 minutes before. This time we made it across without incident, and we found the bodies of the two VC runners on the other side of the dike where they dropped.

Our air assets were gone but they somehow scraped up a Huey slick and a LOCH to ferry us back to Tan Tru making multiple trips back and forth bringing in ten men per lift. They took two of us in a LOCH and overloaded the Huey with eight troops instead of the usual six and finally got everyone back to the fire base within an hour.

August 1968
Some Members of the Third Platoon

Far left: Snyder
Seated: Joe Johnson
Tall soldier in center: Wayne Pope
Giving the Finger: Spaulding
Behind Spaulding: Robert Jordan
Second from right: Ronald Cavett
Far right: McMahon

40   September Sorrows

In September it seemed Charlie Company had more new replacements than at any time since I had been there. They were good soldiers but many of them were still too new to understand and know that you didn't have to do exactly as you were told, that you needed to think independently before acting. This meant you needed to ask questions and always look for alternative ways to accomplish objectives in the field.

On one night in early September Charlie Company was part of an operation where the higher ups ordered us to link up with a company of the 2nd of the 39th who were dropped on the other side of a wood line to cordon off enemy troops we had exchanged fire with earlier.

Situated behind a paddy dike that paralleled the wooded area there was an open rectangular rice paddy about two thirds the size of a football field between us and the VC. The unit of the 2nd of the 39th was on the adjacent flank of the wood line to our left. We could link up with them by moving left along the dike to its corner then following it forward to the link up point.

There was ample moonlight that would enable the VC to spot us if we cut diagonally across the paddy for the link up but that was exactly what we were ordered to do by the unit commander flying above in the C&C helicopter. The Third Platoon was on the point for the link up and we knew it was stupid to cross the open paddy so we flat out refused to do it. The unit commander up above was watching us through a Starlight Scope. We were told he wanted us to cross diagonally to draw enemy fire so he could pinpoint their location from above. Our squad leader and our point man both refused, and we simply headed toward the link up along the dike instead.

Watching from above, the furious colonel (whichever which one he was) demanded to be put on our squad's radio frequency to speak directly to our squad leader. When he came on the radio our squad leader told the commander up in the sky "...it's really dark down here and we were doing the best we can to find our way". That was that. We made the link up safely doing it our own way, and fuck the colonel.

That was an example of how a lot of us were surviving our tours. But with so many newer troops in Charlie Company with just two or three months in country it seemed to me we were getting into too many unnecessary jams out in the field, and with every passing day I was getting more and more nervous and just plain scared about what seemed like too much unnecessary carelessness.

On September 3rd Charlie Company suffered one KIA. Ronal Wayne Neal, 21, a veteran combat medic from Rockport, Indiana who was already into his eighth month in country. On September 5th, we lost four killed, ambushed moving toward a wood line. Albert Rickerson, 27 was from Swainsboro, Georgia starting his third month. Robert Jordan Jr., 20 was from Paris, Illinois with two months in country. Fred Rugh, 18 was from Youngstown, Ohio with two months in country. The fourth was Raymond Stolpa, 20 from Golden, Colorado who had been in country for less than two months.

Jordan was in the third platoon, and I cannot remember much about Stolpa and Rugh, only that I was acquainted with them but never had enough time to get to know either one of them very much. It was a time for me when I didn't allow myself to get to know a lot of the new kids in the platoon very well, as I was getting more rattled by the stress of combat and I had lost so many friends that I began to avoid getting close to the new guys.

Geoff Kerber was the one guy that I spent a lot of time with, and he was now the leader in the platoon that was taking charge of the new ones. But Jordan, the guy from

Illinois was a smart kid and one of the new arrivals that I came to know.

After the disaster on September 5th Ronnie Cavett came into the platoon shack at Tan Tru looking like hell. Cavett was still pissed off at me about my attitude since I had returned from my body escort job. He had been through the hell of the mess in June and never missed a day in the field. But when he walked into the shack that day I knew there was something really wrong with him. His skin was yellow and he was sick. I urged him to get over to sick call and get checked out and he headed to the battalion Aid Station.

He had somehow contracted a case of very infectious hepatitis. The medics at the Aid Station immediately knew how sick he was and he was flown out of Tan Tru to a hospital at Bien Hoa and then ferried to Japan and then back to the states. He never returned to Vietnam. Now Bill Sommers and Ronnie Cavett, the two guys I came into Tan Tru with were both gone.

The night before Jordan was killed it was September Fourth, my twentieth birthday. The platoon had the night off so Jordan and I went over to the HHC shack of the battalion medics. They had a trash can full of iced down beers and we spent the night there with the medics drinking and listening to music on AFVN, and pledging to each other that we were all going to make it back to the world.

The next morning, still celebrating, I went to the Aid Station on sick call complaining that I needed glasses. Jordan went out on operations with the company. The doc at the Aid Station sent me into Dong Tam to see the eye doctor. I came back to Tan Tru two days later with a prescription for corrective lenses. It was when I got back that I learned that Jordan and the other three guys had been killed on September 5th.

In an infantry platoon you make lifelong friends and you bond with other soldiers like no other experience a man can have. But at the same time it is the loneliest experience a person can ever endure. No matter how close you become you are in the end on your own. Robert Jordan was one of those guys that was smart, and careful, but the odds were not good in that situation and they can catch up with anyone. To this day I often think about Robert Jordan Jr. from Paris Illinois. And I remember the night we drank together and shared our hopes of survival together on the night before he walked point into a wood line and was cut down.

41 The Gunfighter Goes Down

Four days later, late in the afternoon of September 9th Charlie Company was sent out to secure a downed helicopter. We saddled up and we were flown out to the wreckage. All that was left of the burned LOCH when we arrived was a black smoking spot of melted metal next to a grove of thick Nipa Palm. The VC who had shot down the ship were gone when we arrived, and as we took up our positions around the wreckage word cracked over the radio that the downed LOCH was none other than Colonel Henry Emerson's personal scouting and recon chopper. The "Gunfighter" had gone down, somewhat injured but alive along with the pilot and his Man Friday.

There was a shared sense of relief among the troops there that Colonel Henry Emerson was headed out. As our Brigade Commander he pushed us to the limits and beyond and everyone hoped that whoever replaced him would be an improvement. I thought about the turnover. Older guys were getting off the line replaced by kids just like me; platoon members were wounded or killed leaving the rest of us there. Our officers, company commanders and platoon leaders came and went, wounded or killed, and still there were people just like me left humping the paddies eight months into our tours.

I thought again about Bill Sommers, hospitalized up at Cam Ranh Bay, and about Cavett, who had been so pissed off at me because I didn't want anything to do with the whole fucking mess, now gone too. And I thought about how pleased I was that Colonel Emerson was going to be out of here.

A couple days later we were out on another operation when we came upon a wood line again and we were hit with small arms fire. We had artillery support which pounded the wood line ahead of us and two Cobra gun ships that poured mini gunfire on a couple of hooches that were the source of some enemy fire. The two hooches were on the border of the wood line and we were finally able to approach the dike located about forty feet in front of them to take up our positions to help seal off the wood line.

We were settled down behind the dike where a guy sixty feet to my right had just stuffed a mosquito net up into his helmet to keep it dry as he was lying prone behind the dike to settle in like the rest of us, when an AK-47 suddenly opened from the hooch right in front of him. It was a hooch that we thought had been cleared. A couple of the rounds ripped into his helmet, but because the mosquito net was stuck up there making his steel pot three inches higher than his head, he only received some shrapnel wounds to the back of his legs from the helmet steel. To look at his helmet you would swear the guy wearing it was killed.

We immediately called for one of the Cobras to hit the hooch. A Cobra made a turn behind us and took a beeline toward the hooch, but it had the wrong hooch in its sites and it was coming in toward the hooch directly in front of my position firing rockets that came from behind just over our heads. The rockets would be spreading shrapnel on four of us who were just then making our way forward.

Seeing the Cobra coming toward the wrong hooch we all jumped down into a four foot by four foot uncovered one foot deep former VC bunker depression twenty feet in front of the hooch and pressed our heads to the dirt. The Cobra was on target, hitting the hooch with three or four rockets but one of the guys across from me in the hole caught a small shrapnel fragment in his shoulder.

The radios all called out "Check fire! Check fire"! The Cobra pilot was pretty shook up but relieved to find we were OK. He came on to our company's PRC 25 radio frequency to personally apologize. Then he made a second run on the correct hooch. When his rockets hit, it exploded and the hooch immediately burst into fire with secondary explosions. It had been stocked with enemy weapons.

The four of us who had been in the line of the wrong hooch then made our way to the left side of the wood line a few minutes later. The guy who had been hit was okay and we took up a position where we were told to hold while artillery was called in to pepper the entire wood line. They were firing from our left to a target about 250 feet away and we could hear the artillery rounds soaring above us as the rounds came down, shaking the ground as they landed. We were now on the left side of the wood line with two of us on the outside of a dike and two others on the other side. We were on a corner of the dike where it bent around the side of the wood line. We could hear the rounds fire and moments later we watched the rounds soar above us. But on the second or third volley something went wrong.

The arty guys loaded each shell with a powder charge which was one to seven. Seven bags of powder for each canister were separated by stitching. The arty guys loaded each canister with what was called a charge one to a charge seven. If it was a charge three the guy loading the canister tore off four bags and left three. It was simple math. But if one of the guys on a gun accidentally tore off five bags instead of three it left only two bags in the canister. If this happened the round would come up short. It was called a short round.

We were taking cover by the dike and five guns fired at a time. This time four rounds soared across us but the fifth one was short and it was coming down right on top of us. An artillery round makes a menacing sound as it soars down on a man. We all found out on this one. The round landed less than ten feet away and plowed down into soft mud on the opposite side of the dike from me. When it exploded the noise and concussion left the four of us unable to hear a sound for twenty minutes.

I came up over the dike and asked the two guys on the other side if they were okay. I saw their lips move but I could not hear them even though they were yelling at me from eighteen inches away. None of us could hear a sound, only the ringing in our ears. After a few moments one of the guys on the other side of the dike where the round exploded pulled himself up on the dike. He was hurt. A medic came over and we pulled his pants down to reveal that half of one side of his buttocks was laid open with a ten inch gash that was open and bleeding.

The medic tended to him and gave him a shot of morphine as the three of us stood by behind the dike. It took about fifteen minutes before the euphoria of the morphine came over him. A dust off was coming in. As our hearing slowly returned we sat there together and rejoiced with him that he was finished with the war and getting out of this fucked up place. We lit smokes and celebrated right then and there, never to see one another again.

42   Unnecessary Losses

The orders declaring me an E-3 Private First Class never came down into the battalion. The company clerk told me I was still a Spec Four and that maybe Major Loeffke had just sent me a message and didn't really bust me. It didn't matter to me because in the entire scope of things I didn't care about anything other than getting my ass out of Vietnam in one piece. They put me in for a promotion E-5 but I didn't really care about that either. More and more I was slipping through the cracks. Whoever was in charge of the third platoon at the time thought I was off the line or on the line and there were days when the platoon or company went out and no one even came around to find me. In any case I went out most of the time and when we hit the paddies I became a platoon of one.

It was on a late September under a monsoon overcast wet damp morning we were preparing for another Eagle Flight when Bill Sommers came limping in. He had been gone since June. When we saw each other we performed a quick exchange of where you been and how are you. It was great to see him. I told him about Cavett and asked how he was doing and I quickly realized the man could hardly walk, still healing from shrapnel wounds with several pieces still embedded in him. Then he told me he had been cleared by the docs up at Cam Ranh Bay for duty. I couldn't believe it. By this time I couldn't care less about what the company commander, the first sergeant or anyone else thought of me.

Sommers was the quiet farm boy from Wisconsin who rarely spoke up about anything. But by this point in his tour he was silently consumed with rage, so disgusted with the war and the brass that he couldn't even speak. At the hospital at Cam Ranh Bay he had refused the Purple Heart (his second one) some officer tried to hand to him. Now he was back at Tan Tru, declared fit for duty when he could hardly walk.

Sommers was too pissed off to even speak so I went with him up to the Orderly Room and up to confront First Sergeant Bobo who was sitting behind his desk. I asked him as the company clerk stood by what was going on. I told him Sommers came into Tan Tru with me that he had been wounded twice already, and could barely walk. I told him if they tried to order Sommers back to the field I wouldn't be surprised if every man in the third platoon would refuse to ever pick up a rifle again. He relented and told Sommers he was off the line for the time being and they would find some other duties for him.

I walked down out of the Orderly Room with Bill, still stunned that some military doc had actually given him a clean bill of health. I figured he must have really pissed them off up there at the hospital.

Through the month of October I continued to try to make myself as useless as possible. New guys came in and, even though I had just turned twenty and most of the replacements were older than me, they seemed terribly young and unprepared for what was ahead of them. On the 15th of September four more guys in Charlie Company died in a firefight, and we had a KIA on the 21st, John Mc Gehee who was a really great kid from San Jose, California and a young barber back in the states. Mc Gehee quickly became the barber for Charlie Company too. But he died in a firefight while still five days short of completing his first month in Vietnam. We lost another man on the 23rd, and still another on the 24th. Twelve were dead in the month of September of 1968 in six different days, in six different firefights.

Now, as I try to recount the months of September through November my memories blur. Ed Crane had made it out in one piece and In October the Cleary's, Holloway's, Joe Johnson's and Ryan's, the October group survivors were all headed home, having completed their tours. I knew I was getting close to getting off the line. With the October guys gone I was now one of the longest surviving members of Charlie Company still on the line and every time I went to the field I hoped it might be my last.

I also continued to try to help counsel the new arrivals. Without question my biggest failure in that department was the case of a young PFC from Kentucky named Jimmy Wayne Hardwick. He had arrived in Vietnam on October 4th and found his way to Charlie Company around mid October. When I talked with him on the day of his arrival he told me he was upset about having been assigned to the Ninth Infantry Division. He wore an airborne badge so I assumed he had attended the airborne training school at Fort Benning, Georgia following his AIT.

When he was ordered to Vietnam he had been bound and determined to get assigned to the 101st Airborne Division. But here he was, stuck down in the Mekong Delta with the Ninth. He was also determined to go out and kill some Viet Cong as soon as he could, in spite of my counsel on how best to stay alive. He was a pretty hard headed case. On October 25th he was cut down by AK-47 fire in his first and last firefight.

November finally arrived and I was still on the line. On one company operation early that month the company found itself backing up the 2nd of the 39th again, dropped in and setting up a blocking force in a wet rice paddy by a wood line next to a blue ("blue" is what we called rivers or canals). I was standing next to an artillery forward observer Lieutenant when we saw a lift of choppers ferrying in our Bravo Company on the other side of the blue directly across from our position. As they came in they started to take fire. In response their door gunners opened up on the wood line.

But there was a problem. We were in their direct line of fire and found ourselves hitting the mud for cover from our own people. I remember thinking as the bullets cracked past my ears that I had been in the field too long for this kind of nonsense. Radio men were screaming "Check Fire…Check Fire!" into their handsets as the firing finally abated with Bravo's insertion on the other side.

Crap like this was happening with increasing frequency it seemed to me. A few days later we actually got into a two minute fire fight with Bravo Company on another operation. Somebody thought they saw movement in a wood line and took a couple of shots. The next thing we knew Bravo Company, patrolling about three hundred meters on the other side of the wood line opened up on full automatic in our direction. No one had bothered to inform either company of the position of the other. Fortunately nobody got hurt, but it took a couple of minutes before they got it stopped.

The stress was manifested in a number of incidents in Charlie Company and throughout the other companies in the battalion as well in the latter months of 1968.

While seated on the Tan Tru chopper pad in the center seat of one of the ten idling Hueys one morning just about to lift off for an Eagle Flight a Spec Four by the of Rizzo who was an M-79 grenadier from the other squad of the Third Platoon accidently discharged his weapon's shot gun round through the roof of the aircraft, blowing a hole through its top disabling the Huey.

The next day Division HQ issued a directive that all M-79's were to be broken open while troops were idling on pick-up zones.

About that same time the M-60 machine gunner from the same squad who was new to his job accidently shot himself in the thigh one afternoon with his holstered forty-five caliber side arm while we were on stand-by at Tan Tru.

Machine gunners were issued the pistols for use in close ground combat situations, but they were really more of a convenience to carry in base camp where everyone carried a weapon at all times. A couple days later every machine gunner in the battalion was ordered to turn in his side arm.

Nineteen sixty-eight was taking its toll on the U.S. military. Before the year would be over almost 17,000 Americans would die that year in Vietnam, twice as many as died there in 1967. In 1968 the President of the United States would choose not to run for reelection, the Paris Peace talks became a joke, the Democratic Convention in Chicago would spark riots, and young people were taking to the streets in cities and towns throughout the country. Robert Kennedy and Martin Luther King Jr. were assassinated, and returning American troops were changing out of their uniforms as soon as they got home lest they be spat upon by an ignorant and angry public.

The toll it took upon units in the field like Charlie Company and the rest of the 2nd of the 60th was becoming apparent. The company was competent with good leadership early in 1968 but by the end of the year unnecessary mistakes and tactical misjudgments were killing too many young men.

I have long heard that in other infantry units throughout Vietnam infantry soldiers stayed in the field right up to the final days of their tours. I do not dispute this is true, I only know there were very few troops in our unit who spent their entire tour on the line. Perhaps there were others but Joe Johnson is the only member of our third platoon I can recall spending his entire year on the line, but he was most certainly the exception to the rule.

Stateside infantry companies were about 120 to 130 men. During the bulk of my tour our companies had maybe 65 to 75 men on the average to give a generous estimate, and this included the headquarters platoon. There were three rifle platoons that needed to muster at least 56 men between them to meet the 60 man threshold for Eagle Flight air assaults. The other four slots consisted of the company commander, his RTO and the artillery forward observer and his RTO.

Given the size of our companies, and with the casualty rates experienced in the 2nd of the 60th in 1968, the completion of an entire year out in the field meant that a troop had a better than 30% chance of being killed, and a better than 100% chance of being either killed or wounded. Everyone understood this and that is why I believe that higher- ups in our unit found duties off the line for most soldiers when they reached the eighth or ninth month of their tours.

I suspect another reason was soldiers who survived well into their tours became more and more useless, cynical and jaded and could easily affect troop morale for new replacements vital to the mission. I have no doubt I was looked upon by higher ups as one of these characters.

One of the new replacements assigned to Charlie Company in the fall was a young man I will call "Sidney" (not his real name). When "Sidney" arrived many of us thought he was putting on an act to get reassigned off the line. He behaved like a moron with a childlike manner.

Turned out we were wrong. Unbeknownst to us at the time, John McNamara's Pentagon had established a program called Project 100,000. It established lower physical and mental standards for the military that allowed individuals who would have been rejected for military service to be drafted.

"Sidney" was one of these young men. He was assigned to the Third Platoon, and was sent out on operations just like the rest of us. Shortly after his arrival he saw his first action. During the firefight he had to be physically pulled down behind the dike by his platoon mates to keep him from getting shot, and he had no idea which direction to point his weapon.

After this initial action he was assigned only to pull perimeter bunker guard at Tan Tru. His first time performing this duty he sat atop the bunker facing inward toward the base camp. When asked what the hell he was doing he replied he was looking for the officer of the day coming around on his nightly bunker inspection so that he would be able to tell him he was alert and on duty.

Following this he was assigned as a helper of sorts in the supply shack. He finished his tour of duty there, but not before he earned a Purple Heart when he sustained shrapnel wounds to one of his legs in a mortar attack.

The worst example of chaos in the platoon I witnessed came one night in October when the platoon was given a night off following a Bushmaster operation.

One of the men in our squad, a Native American, who shall remain nameless here, was drinking that night, as were many of us. Like Van Etsitty, this fellow had almost no tolerance for alcohol, except that in his case, unlike Etsitty, he became extremely belligerent following the consumption of just one or two beers. This same individual, when sober was a great, well liked soldier who got along well with everyone.

As he became drunker and drunker he walked around the platoon hooch trying to pick fights with platoon mates. On this particular night Wayne Pope, who by this time had begun to display serious signs that he was mentally falling apart from months of steady combat, was resting on his cot. Pope had taken to the habit of liberating bottles of Vietnamese rice wine from hoochs out in the field and he was polishing off a bottle of the stuff that night.

Pope was sitting back on his cot located next to the door on one end of the platoon hooch when the soldier walked up and slapped his head, trying to start a fight. Pope, despite being three sheets to the wind, stood up, grabbed the man by his collar and literally tossed him out the door on to the mud outside. Those of us inside hoped this would be the end of this madness for the night. We were set to go out on Eagle Flights at 0800 the next morning and most of us just wanted to get some sleep by this time.

I laid back on my own cot and tried to doze off. The Tan Tru generator had shut down earlier and the only light remaining inside was from a few candles and flashlights. But just thirty minutes later the soldier came back looking for Pope, but this time he was armed with an M-16, fully loaded. He was so drunk he walked right past Pope's cot, halfway through the hooch and stopped beside another soldier who was sound asleep.

In the semi-darkness of the platoon hooch he stood over the unsuspecting soldier two cots away from mine, and pointed the weapon with the end of the barrel two inches away from the sleeping man's head. He locked and loaded the M-16, flipped it off safe, put his finger on the trigger and just stood there. He was completely out of his mind, not having any idea of what he was doing. Then he yelled out for Pope.

Wayne Pope, sitting six cots away responded, "I'm over here you drunken Indian!" Hearing this the Indian walked over to Pope and pointed the M-16 at Pope's chest. In an instant Pope ripped the rifle out of his hands, dropped the magazine out of the weapon, ejected the chambered round and threw the Indian out the door and into the mud outside once more.

After witnessing all this from but a few feet away I found myself shaking like a leaf with anger. This kind of crazy stupidity would never have happened in the Third Platoon during the early months of my tour. I got so angry that I got up, walked outside and went looking for the Indian myself.

I found him outside next to the company ammo bunker with two or three soldiers vainly pleading with him to give it up and hit his cot for some sleep. I had had enough so I confronted him myself, but instead of talk I simply began to throw fist after fist planting round house punches on both sides of his jaw. He grabbed the front of my jungle fatigue shirt holding on to me as I hit again and again as I was yelling at him to let go of me. After a dozen or so punches he finally let go, fell back on the ground and stayed there.

The next morning after eating breakfast at the Tan Tru mess hall I found the Indian back at Charlie Company as he was washing up as we were preparing to go out on the day's operation. I was apprehensive because he was a pretty strong and tough customer, but he approached me and quietly thanked me. He didn't have a mark on his face but he could barely mumble his words. He told me he heard from others that I had beat the shit out him last night. And then he asked me to do the same thing if he ever behaved that way again.

By the middle of November I had finally outlasted the higher ups that disliked me and my lousy attitude. When there came a point when a job off the line at Tan Tru became available there was really no one else to consider for it, and the old leaders in the company that would have kept me out humping the paddies until my DEROS were gone back to the states.

They needed another body to man the battalion base camp's radar look out tower over in Echo Company. The job was with a small group that manned the tower twenty-four hours a day. The tower was 20 feet high and sand bagged bottom, sides and top. So around the 20th of November I was assigned to Echo Company. I was off the line. No more Eagle Flights and no more LZ's. It was goodbye to Charlie Company.

43 Off the Line and Cannon Duty

The job with Echo Company was a great relief. I soon discovered that a job off the line meant I was now on the roster to perform KP (kitchen patrol) duty at the Tan Tru mess hall, and since I was now staying at base camp at night for the first time I got to experience the periodic mortar attacks Tan Tru absorbed a couple nights a week. Since I had always been out in the bush at night before this I was almost always absent when these attacks happened.

They usually lasted for about five minutes with five or ten 82mm mortars dropped around the camp around midnight. We slept in bunkers at night so for the most part they were just a nuisance.

When I had KP duty I returned to my old specialty from my days in training at Fort Ord and Fort Polk. I once again perfected my skills as a pots and pans specialist. Pots and pans duty was considered the most miserable KP job but I didn't mind the work because I always got to arrive latest to KP and none of the cooks fucked with me. I did my job alone outside and began counting the days I had left in Vietnam.

My time on the Tan Tru watch tower was memorable but short. On December twelfth orders for me came down from division headquarters assigning me to a temporary duty station (TDY) to the 1st of the 11th Artillery. By this time I was counting days… 57 left to go. I was what they called a "two digit midget".

On the morning of December 13th I cleaned out my wooden foot locker in the Echo Company hooch next to the lookout tower outside and next to the base perimeter and gathered up my gear. There wasn't much of importance there except for the four inch screen Crowne black and white TV with AM/FM radio I had purchased at the China Fleet Club when I was on R&R in Hong Kong. It was powered by nine

"D" batteries that gave it about four hours of TV time. The Army supply shack had tons of batteries that I used for free.

I hopped the supply truck out of Tan Tru for Dong Tam where I was ordered to report. In the morning I waited with a small convoy readying to head out of Tan Tru at 0800 hours that morning. The 12 klicks of Tan Tru Road had to be cleared of mines and bad guys every morning, and on this day there were hay bales and mines planted half way to Tan An. It took until noon before the convoy got the green light to head toward Tan An and the main highway and on to My Tho and Dong Tam.

Upon arrival at Dong Tam that afternoon I learned that more than a dozen other infantrymen from other units of the Ninth Division had the same orders as me. Comparing notes we found that each one of us had less than sixty days remaining on our tours. I recognized one of the guys there who I had taken AIT with back at D/4/3 in Fort Polk. We surmised the division needed artillery personnel so they decided to transfer infantrymen who were nearing the completion of their tours temporary duty (TDY) to help out at various artillery units.

None of us complained. Working on an artillery battery was a hell of a lot better duty than serving in an infantry line company. I was assigned to a battery of the 1/11th Artillery that was operating out of Fire Base Moore on Highway 4 east of the Pink Palace. I had been through there before with Charlie Company. When we were at the Pink Palace we staged quite a few night ambush patrols out of Fire Base Moore.

I had no artillery training on the 105 mm Howitzer but it didn't take much training to help on fire missions. My job was to count off the number and load powder charges that went into the artillery canister for each round. Not exactly rocket science but it was important to get the number of powder charges right. I knew from firsthand experience what happened if the round was shorted a charge and so I was very careful to get it right.

Life on an artillery battery was OK. Each morning a deuce and a half truck would be loaded with artillery rounds and all the other equipment we would need for the day's operation. We would tow a 105mm Howitzer behind the truck. One man rode shotgun up front with the driver while the rest of us piled on in back. With the 1/11th we towed out three guns heading down the road to a destination where we were close enough to support infantry operations.

We would set up the guns in a dry paddy or driveway next to the highway and wait to be called for a fire mission. The artillery boys had a system. They set up the guns and got ready for the fire mission call. In the meantime they paid some little Vietnamese kid that inevitably wandered by a dollar and a half to bring back a block of ice. When the ice arrived they pulled a couple of cases of beer off the back of the truck and iced them down. Then we would kick back over some cold ones and wait.

Riding out in the morning and back to the fire base at night we often had a few shots popped at us, but they were always from long range and constituted little more than a nuisance. But the drivers always boogied on at a pretty good pace down the highway and the little Librettas and other vehicles carrying the local Vietnamese traffic gave us a wide berth.

On occasion we would have to stay out all night camped along the highway to support infantry operations. When this happened an infantry company would be sent out to provide perimeter security for us.

On the battery I was assigned there was a platoon leader Lieutenant who I soon discovered had a problem with me. He didn't like having a guy working on one of his guns who had no artillery training, and more than that he didn't like having a guy wearing a Combat Infantryman's Badge working under his authority. The guy had yet to serve his time as a Forward Observer (FO) with an infantry company and he clearly resented my presence there.

For my part, I couldn't care less about that kind of crap and I actually went out of my way to show him deference. In fact I kind of felt sorry for him knowing he was soon headed to field duty with the infantry. Nevertheless one day as we were set up with three guns out on Highway Four waiting around for a fire mission he ordered me over to where he was standing and chatting with the other members of my gun. I came over and he asked me where I was from. I told him California and he made some crack about California hippies. I was used to good-natured jive about California hippies and I casually replied that sure, I knew a few hippies back home but I never had the time to become one myself.

Then he told me in a stern voice that I was dismissed. I looked at him somewhat quizzically and said "yes sir" and I turned to walk away. But before I could go he stopped me and told me I forgot to salute him. At this point I had no doubt that he was making an example of me before my gun mates to assert his authority.

In the field in Vietnam you never saluted an officer. It was prohibited because the enemy could identify officers and target them if they were saluted. So I was astounded that he wanted me to salute him. I said to him "We're in the field, Sir". He said he knew where we were and ordered me to salute him anyway. So I saluted him, he returned the salute, having made his point, and I turned away and left as the other guys on the gun looked on in silence.

Now, at this point in my tour I was operating with a pretty short fuse when it came to this kind of bullshit. I had been through too much to put up with this from some punk second Lieutenant. So I wandered out to the third gun that was set up farthest from the highway where I loitered alone smoking cigarettes. Finally, about two hours after the salute incident, the Lieutenant came by making his rounds. Now it was just him and me.

As he approached me I calmly said, "Hey Lieutenant, I want you to know something." He walked up to me and I said, "If you ever pull that kind of crap on me again, I might have to kill you. I won't kill you in front of the other guys though. I'll have to kill you when no one else will know that I killed you".

Of course, in truth, I would not really kill him. But he didn't know that. His face turned bright red and he turned around and walked away from me without saying a word. I could see that I had made my point.

A couple days later he became sick with some tropical disease and was taken away. He never returned, at least not before I had left the Battery.

44   A Christmas Truce and Hong Kong Revisited

I had taken my R&R in August but I still had a seven day leave coming to me before I left Vietnam. I put in for the leave for the early part of January so that I could return to Vietnam with only a couple of weeks left to go when I returned. As Christmas of 1968 approached we found ourselves setting up on a daily basis in different spots on Highway 4 east of Fire Base Moore. The big Bob Hope USO show was coming to Dong Tam on Christmas Day. Our six gun mates on our 105 Howitzer had two slots among us for the show and it was decided to draw straws to see who would go. I drew a short straw and I didn't mind a bit. I was getting short in my tour and two fellows with more than eight months left drew the long straws. They needed the entertainment more than I did and I was more than happy for them to go.

In 1968 the high command in Saigon declared a 24-hour Christmas truce. All operations were to cease at 1800 hours on Christmas Eve and all units were ordered to base camps by 1800 hours to stand down.

When the magic hour arrived our three guns were just completing a fire mission. We quickly loaded the trucks and hitched up the cannons for the thirty minute ride back in to Fire Base Moore. We began our little caravan back in at about 1750 hours so we were actually on the road when the truce went into effect.

There were some Roman Catholics in the little villages along Highway 4 and we passed a couple of Catholic churches along the way back. Outside the churches little Vietnamese children were dressed up for the holiday and we tossed candies to them as we drove past them. It was really very touching. A couple of kilometers off in the distance at precisely 1800 hours I watched as two F104 or F100 jets were conducting a close support bombing mission pulled up, did a circle over the area and headed back in to their base. It made for a very memorable and special Christmas memory for me.

A couple days following the arrival of 1969 I headed in to Dong Tam where I caught a Caribou flight to Saigon and Camp Alpha, the staging area for R&R and leave. When I arrived they announced the first flights out were for Hong Kong. Many of the other leave destinations, Kuala Lumpur, Bangkok, Taipei, Australia, and the like were more popular than Hong Kong, and I had already visited Hong Kong on my R&R. I didn't care. If Hong Kong was the first available I took it.

Once again I was fitted for Khakis and taken to Bien Hoa for a flight to Hong Kong. It was the same routine...head to the approved bar, select the approved female companion and go to the approved hotel. This time I stayed with the first young lady for two days then I returned her to the bar. I decided to spend a day by myself.

That night I took the Star Ferry over to Hong Kong Island (my hotel was on the Kowloon side) and over to the Hong Kong Hilton. I took the elevator to the restaurant on the top floor with a beautiful view of the city. There I ordered a New York steak dinner. With a couple of beers to go with it the bill came to about six dollars. Hong Kong was unbelievably inexpensive.

After dinner I sat at the bar where I met a couple of Aussie soldiers also on leave from Vietnam, and later had some drinks with a Green Beret. The Green Beret needed to pick up some porn movies to bring back to Vietnam to trade for supplies he wanted for his unit.

The Green Berets operated independently and on their own. I had once witnessed a Chinook helicopter land on an isolated part of Dong Tam when I was there a day. I spoke to a couple of them for a few of minutes when they asked me for directions to the division's Post Exchange. They had about $500 in cash and they were there to wheel and deal for supplies to take back to their outpost. They were interested in gasoline, portable generators, portable refrigerators, steaks, booze and stereos.

About an hour later they drove up in a deuce and a half truck filled with goods. They not only took the goods, they took the deuce and a half too! They strapped the loaded truck up to the hook of the Chinook and off they flew. Those guys knew how to operate.

So I understood the Green Beret at the hotel bar. He asked me to go with him on his porn movie search mission as a sort of back up and I agreed. Together we went back to Kowloon, grabbed a non-authorized taxi and drove in circles all over the city. The driver took us to two different apartment buildings. In each we took an elevator up to a room. Inside we sat in folding chairs and previewed sixteen millimeter movies. It was all very secret and no doubt illegal. Turned out the guy didn't like either movie, or the price they were asking. So we left empty-handed. Still, it was something different that I did on my last trip to Hong Kong.

45   Star Trek, Shock and Surprises

Back from Hong Kong in mid January I was counting the days. My DEROS was 8 February, 1969, a date I held in my mind every day since my arrival. I was supposed to report to Division at Dong Tam five days prior to DEROS on February.3rd. This meant I had to return to Tan Tru, my permanent duty station by February 1st to turn in my combat gear before going to Dong Tam. I was only two weeks away from the start of my journey home at Tan Tru.

At Fire Base Moore we still headed out every morning with the three guns, traveling over Highway 4 to each day's destination. I had my four inch TV with me at FSB Moore. One night with about a week left to go we were ordered to stay out all night with the guns beside the highway. As usual an infantry company came out to provide night security. On this night we were set up adjacent to one of the ARVN outposts on the highway.

As night fell I placed the little TV up on some ammo boxes to permit a half dozen guys to watch an episode of Star Trek playing on AFVN TV. About half way through the episode an ARVN jeep with its lights on drove past us down the highway. In my entire time in Vietnam I had never seen a vehicle driving at night like this. It appeared it was only going from an ARVN compound across the highway to some village buildings down the road.

Just as it passed our position it was fired at with a rocket propelled grenade (RPG) and AK 47 fire broke out. Tracers were passing over us and I found it ridiculous that I had to jump up and turn off the little TV before heading for my rifle and hunker down. It was all over in two minutes, but it was a reminder that I was not out of the woods yet.

February 1st finally arrived and I bid goodbye to my friends at the 1st of the 11th Artillery and caught a ride into

Dong Tam followed by another to Tan Tru the next day. On February 2nd I rolled into Tan Tru for the last time. When I got there I was surprised with the news that Tan Tru had been hit by a ground attack on the night of December 13th. It was the day I had left.

I went over to Echo Company where my last hooch was to find the corrugated roof above my cot half blown away. My wooden foot locker was still there with dozens of shrapnel holes punched through it. A mortar shell or RPG had done the damage. I shook my head thinking about how many times I had escaped shit like that by sheer timing. I had left that afternoon and the ground attack happened that very night.

Tan Tru was undergoing big changes too. Throughout the base camp the wooden platoon hooches we all used were all being reinforced by sandbagging. Where we once had canvas tops or corrugated roofs there were now heavy framed sand bagged structures.

I went over to Charlie Company and found the supply shack. I told them I was going to DEROS out and I was there to turn in my gear. It was there that I turned in my steel pot and helmet liner for a bush hat. I was kind of in shock to be back at Tan Tru and to think I was really going home.

When I turned in my steel pot I removed the helmet liner inside and took off the cloth camouflage cover. It had the green wet season camouflaged side out, just as it was when it was issued to me back in June when I had returned from Danny Powell's escort duty. When I pulled the helmet liner out from the steel pot I discovered an American dollar bill inside between the liner and steel pot. And when I opened the cloth camouflaged helmet cover and turned it out I found some writing on it. It said in big black inked letters: Struthers, Ohio.

I was shocked to find I had been wearing Sgt. Charles Huzico's helmet ever since I came back in June and I never knew it. It was the very helmet liner and steel pot he had been wearing when he was killed and it had been issued to me just a couple days after he had died wearing it, when I returned to Tan Tru. The dollar bill hidden inside was a lucky charm that didn't work for him. I guessed it had worked for me. I was stunned.

I visited the third platoon hooch where I had first taken up residency almost a year ago. I walked in and was met by a couple of soldiers who had no idea who I was. I told them I was a member of the third platoon and they just looked at me like a stranger. I asked if they knew where Wayne Pope was and one of them told me he thought he was out with Echo Company's mortar platoons on the other side of the fire base's artillery guns.

I wandered my way over there and found Pope. He was a mental wreck, and he seemed to me to be on another wave length. We shook hands and I told him I was leaving the next day. He seemed not to even comprehend me. I don't know what had happened to him, but he seemed content to be off the line and working on the 81mm mortar unit, a unit that did nothing terribly vital at Tan Tru. It seemed to me that it was mostly a holding job for people no longer considered useful.

I was getting paranoid about being in Tan Tru for my last night and hardly knowing a soul. I tried to find Geoff Kerber but was told he was out on a patrol. I went over to the Tan Tru EM Club and had a couple of beers. I wanted to find the safest place I could find to spend the night.

I found that Bravo Company had completed the renovation and sandbagging of one of their platoon hoochs. I went over there to find a safe place to sack out. I walked inside and found two black soldiers there who asked who I was. I told them I was looking for a cot to sleep on and that I was leaving the next day. I found an empty cot and sacked out.

At three in the morning I was awakened by fifty caliber machine gun fire from the perimeter bunker right outside. People were grabbing their weapons and running for the perimeter yelling "ground attack!"

I couldn't believe it. Just one more night and let me out of here. But it turned out some quick triggered asshole on the perimeter had fired on one of our own listening posts. When the excitement died down a dust off was headed out to pick up a wounded guy out there who had been hit by our own guys. After that I lay there the rest of the night awake just waiting for the dawn.

When morning finally came I caught a ride out of Tan Tru on a supply truck headed for Dong Tam, but like so many times the road was still closed and not yet cleared.

At noon we headed out and I looked back at Tan Tru for the last time. We made it three quarters of the way to the main highway when we were halted at the last of four road guard posts. The last quarter of the road was still not cleared. I hopped off the truck and walked out to the four man road guard patrol. Who was there but Geoff Kerber?

We talked as we waited for the all clear sign. Kerber told me about a terrible incident that happened on December 28th a little more than a month earlier. He had been walking point as Charlie Company was returning to the village of Thua Thu from an all night operation. As they approached within just a couple hundred meters of the secured village, the force of an explosion knocked Kerber on his back. Before he could get back on his feet a Viet Cong wearing a pith helmet while firing an AK-47 charged across his view no more than ten feet away.

He laid there in the high grass frozen lest the assaulting VC spot him, and there was no way he could pull up his rifle to fire. The VC ambush targeted Charlie Company's CO. Captain William Ferguson was hit by automatic weapons fire. The ambush was over quickly. Geoff made it back to the Captain's position and stood by with him as he died there. Captain Ferguson had more than twelve years of military service and had been in Vietnam for less than two months at the time of his death at the age of thirty-one.

It was good to see Geoff again before I left Vietnam. We talked about me going back to the "world". Geoff was a Sergeant by then and he told me this, "When you get back to the world and people ask you about this place do me a favor. "Don't let anybody slide." (Give them the real story about what is happening in Vietnam.) I promised him I wouldn't and we said goodbye.

46 To the Freedom Bird

On February 3rd I finally arrived at Dong Tam and reported. When I checked in they told me they had been trying to contact me to inform me that my orders for returning to CONUS (Continental United States) had been changed. My DEROS had been moved to February 4th. My airplane home was leaving Bien Hoa the next day.

They quickly handed my orders over along with my Official Army Personnel (201) file. I had to get to Long Bien and get processed out ASAP. With my file in hand I headed directly over to the Dong Tam air strip to catch a Caribou to Long Bien. When I got there I signed up for the next available flight out.

I sat down in the wood frame terminal's tin roofed waiting area and looked through my 201 file. There I found them. My orders for a reduction in rank were there staring right back at me. Major Loeffke had busted me in July, but the paperwork and the order making it official, which I had never seen, was dated 28 December 1968. My date of rank back down to PFC (E-3) was back dated to July.

I shook my head and laughed. I will never know if it was Major Loeffke who personally oversaw the decision to cut my orders long after I was busted in order to prevent any possibility of a subsequent promotion, and after I was sent TDY to the 1/11th Arty, but it was clear that I had been screwed. Someone had made certain that all the requisitions to promote me to E-5 had been denied and I was going to be going home from my tour in Vietnam as a Private First Class.

"This is only fitting", I laughed to myself. There are times in life when you give a crap. This was not one of them. I was going home, surviving my tour and, though pissed, I just didn't care.

When the first Caribou out of Dong Tam landed and readied to take out the next lift of passengers to Long Bien I was not on the list. I would have to wait there for the following flight. I took a seat and prepared to wait the thirty minutes for the next flight. As the departing Caribou crossed the PSP airstrip in front of the small terminal and was lifting away, an RPG rocket landed directly behind it on the PSP airstrip. The VC were trying to shoot it down on its takeoff.

When the rocket landed on the PSP runway fifty meters away, everyone in the terminal scrambled off, including two old Vietnamese women who were sweeping the building with their little half size handled Vietnamese sweeper brooms. I couldn't believe it. I was just about to finally get out of this hell hole and they were trying to shoot down a Caribou.

I was scheduled for a Freedom Bird out of Vietnam in less than twenty-four hours and the bastards out there were still trying to kill me. And I thought to myself, the guys on that plane had no idea the VC had just missed shooting down their aircraft.

After a few minutes everyone but the mama sans returned somewhat shaken to the terminal. I caught the next Caribou out and we departed without incident. Flying away, glancing down out the window, I said goodbye to Dong Tam.

I reached Long Bien, went through the processing, was fitted again with travel khakis, and in the early morning dawn of February 4th I boarded a commercial flight out of Vietnam. I sat in my seat with my head racing over the events of the past year feeling relief, profound sorrow and joy. I was bound for home. With six months remaining in my two year hitch in the Army. The orders in my 201 file told me I was to report to some unit at Fort Ord after I completed my thirty day leave at home.

At least I would be in California to complete my two year hitch, and there was nothing the Army could ever do to me again that would come close to what I had just experienced. As the plane sailed homeward I nodded off for a while. When I woke up I found myself thinking back on some of the events from the year and what it was like when I first found myself at Tan Tru.

The battalion policy there dictated every newly arriving soldier had to spend his first 72 hours inside the perimeter of the fire base before engaging in combat operations out in the field. So instead of going out on ambush patrol with the third platoon my first night there I was assigned to perimeter guard duty on one of the base's bunkers.

It was on the third or fourth bunker south of the base's Tan Tru Road entrance. A heavy wood frame and steel twelve by twelve foot square structure covered with sand bags. Inside you could sit up on a folding chair but the perimeter bunkers there were not tall enough to allow one to stand. You could ladder up top of the bunkers where there were parapets walls two or three sand bags high. All the perimeter bunkers had land line telephone connections to the base's Tactical Operations Center (TAC).

Four troops manned the bunkers each night with one man standing guard for two separate one-hour shifts as the other three slept. For every eight hour guard shift each troop had six hours sleep and two hours guard time. When I arrived for guard duty that first night I introduced myself to the three other troops there and I was impressed that they all had been at Tan Tru for a number of months, sporting faded jungle fatigues, M-16 rifles, loaded magazines and combat steel pot helmets.

There was a good supply of about a dozen fragmentation grenades, a Starlight night scope inside and a blasting cap control for the Claymore mine that was positioned in the concertina wire out front. This particular bunker also featured a tripod mounted M-60 machine gun pointing through a gun port toward the rice paddies outside.

The guys introduced themselves and welcomed me. Then we took our shifts and set in for the night. As the typical new guy I was unable to sleep so I took the first shift, staring intently out to the warm, humid darkness outside the perimeter, watching over the paddies with the Starlight scope, and listening.

The first hour passed uneventfully after which I went to sleep on a poncho liner in the back of the bunker after waking up the number two guy. At around 1200 hours our bunker got a call from the TAC. The commotion awakened me. Someone had reported possible movement out to our front. We were ordered by the TAC to "throw out" a couple dozen rounds from the tripod mounted M-60 out there to stir up whatever it might be. Maybe just be a loose water buffalo, but who knew?

I stood by with my newly minted M-16 rifle in hand, ready for action, as one of the guys fiddled over the M-60. After about two minutes he turned and asked me if I knew how to fire an M-60 machine gun.

I was an infantryman trained at Tigerland on Fort Polk, Louisiana so I knew how operate an M-60 machine gun. I laid the ammo belt into the gun, pulled back the lever, switched the safe to "off", laid the butt of the gun into my shoulder, leveled the barrel and fired off four or five six round bursts.

There was no return fire and it turned out to be nothing of consequence. The rest of the night passed peacefully. Next morning the three comrades thanked me and explained to me how they were glad I had been out on the bunker with them.

That's when I learned the three of them were just cooks. They worked the Tan Tru mess hall. None of them knew anything about infantry weapons beyond the rudiments of their own never fired M-16 rifles. So much for first impressions.

On my second night at Tan Tru, the 72 hour rule was tossed out the window. The third platoon were going out, with me included, to set up a night ambush. On that first night ambush for me we were ordered to first to park ourselves along the shore of the Vam Co River which meandered past the base camp behind a steel shack next to the trash dump by the river.

We were to hold in place there until dark, then board two 18 foot aluminum outboard motor boats and head three kilometers (klicks) down the river to a predetermined spot to set up an ambush for Viet Cong (VC) sampans that might be heading up or down the river at night. An after dark curfew prohibited any movement on the river so any sampan spotted out after dark was presumed to be enemy Viet Cong... and fair game.

It was a stupid and dangerous idea to put troops into outboard aluminum boats and cruise down the river at night, and they all knew it. The patrol that night was led by an E-5 buck sergeant. No officers, no career non-com officers.

As we all sat out there with the garbage waiting for full darkness conversation turned to the stupidity of this ambush assignment. After ruminating on the matter for some time a full consensus was reached to take matters into our own hands. Instead of heading three klicks down the river the patrol assembled into three ambush positions right there next to garbage dump and called in fake sit reps (situation reports) all night from an imaginary location down river.

In the morning we saddled up and walked back over to the Charlie Company huts at Tan Tru. No one upstairs ever knew and no one ever said anything. And all things considered I was grateful to find myself a joining a platoon with some combat vets who knew enough to think for themselves.

Several hours of sleep into the return flight from Vietnam we landed for refueling on Wake Island. We disembarked there for about a half hour and I had the opportunity to walk out to see the bunkers preserved there from the American defenders in World War II. Following the second leg of the flight home we made a second refueling stop at Honolulu where we deplaned again and I got to smell the sweet scent of Hawaiian flowers in the airport.

At the end of the long flight back to the United States we finally landed at Travis AFB in California. It was just as I had done back in June on body escort duty for Danny Powell, only this time I was home from the war for good. It felt wonderful, and I was full of excitement to be coming home.

We were bussed to the Oakland Army Base where I was processed again, and fitted out with Army Dress Greens. This time they sewed on a Ninth Infantry Division patch on my right shoulder to signify that I was a veteran of my combat unit. When they cut us loose to head for the airport we were told to only get taxi rides from authorized and licensed taxi cab drivers. I strolled out to the cab stand and another vet and I shared a ride offered by some college student to San Francisco Airport for $20 bucks.

It was early evening still on the fourth of February when I got to SFO. I booked a flight to LAX and placed a call home. Terry answered and I told him I was coming home and gave him my flight number. I took a seat in the airport and promptly fell asleep again. An airline rep woke me up to get me on my DC-9 flight to LAX.

Once on the plane, still exhausted, I took a seat for the one hour flight to LA. I fell asleep again. The next thing I knew a flight attendant was waking me up in my seat. We were on the ground in LA and the plane was already empty. I grabbed my carry-on bag and headed out of the plane and up the gang way to the terminal.

As I approached the end of the gangway I saw Terry and our next door neighbor, Joe Bradford, waiting there to greet me. I was the last one off the plane and I looked at Terry and Joe and broke out in a big smile. Before I could say a word, Terry placed an index finger over his lips and quietly said "hush"... I looked at him with a quizzical expression as I walked up the ramp.

When I reached him he said quietly: "I only want to hear one word from you!" I said, "what is that?' He said, "Cakewalk".

Understanding Terry's warped sense of humor as only a twin brother can, I sighed, shook my head with a laugh, looked my twin brother in the eye and dutifully replied... "Cakewalk..."

47 A Look Back

It was on the flight home that I had first allowed myself the luxury of contemplating a year's worth of getting my bell rung. I would never let myself go there while I was still in the soup. Little did I realize it then, but it would take more than a life time to unravel and sort through. I remember mulling it over as we were flying home, trying to calculate the number of bullets that had popped over and around my head during twelve months of serving my country in Vietnam. Thousands easy. I could not count the fire fights, the sniping, the harassment fire, the friendly fire, or the shrapnel. And why was I sitting there thinking about that crap anyway? I was going home. My war was over.

I found myself thinking about stupid things like the Charlie Company ammo bunker. Located behind the third platoon hooch back at Tan Tru, it was a sand bagged hole in the ground where all the boxes of M-16 ammunition, fragmentation and concussion grenades, LAW's (light anti-tank weapons) steel green boxes filled with M-16 and belts of M-60 ammo, C-4 plastic explosive bars, and everything else we needed to blow up and shoot things out to the field were stored.

It seemed as if every day we went there and loaded up before heading out to the field. No supervision. Just pull the hatch open and grab what was needed. I sat there in the airplane thinking I never wanted to see that bunker again.

Nine months earlier, back in May, Van Etsitty, my ammo bearer/assistant machine gunner, had followed me down the side of Highway 4 outside the City of My Tho, forty miles southwest of Saigon on a night ambush with no moonlight. He had stopped with the rest of the squad taking a knee on the side the road, waiting out as a flare from a Spooky airplane in the distance lighted our position. When the flare burned down we moved out again. But Etsitty, staring ahead, had lost sight of me. He was the last man in the patrol line and he was staring at a bush next to the road he had mistaken for me crouching down.

The twelve man patrol pushed ahead in the moonless night without him, and when we reached the appointed ambush site two klicks on, the headcount turned up only eleven. Where was Etsitty? So the patrol backtracked looking for him.

Two klicks back retracing our path we found him taking refuge inside a Vietnamese hooch on the side of Highway 4. Sergeant Ryan, our squad leader found him sound asleep there. Etsitty had downed a just a single beer before we set out that night. Some Navajos just aren't built to drink and Etsitty was one. Ryan carefully roused him, brought him around, and we went back to the ambush site with a full contingent, making it there by 1200 hours.

A couple nights before that on another night ambush patrol I had crossed a plank over a Mekong Delta canal carrying the M-60, 300 rounds, 4 grenades, two canteens, and a pack of C-Rations when the 2"X12" plank bridge gave way under my weight in the middle of the ten foot wide canal. One second I was walking across on the plank, the next I was walking on the bottom of the canal with my head submerged.

It was weird. I just kept walking up the muddy bank. Didn't even lose my steel pot helmet. Just kept walking up and out of the canal without losing a step, as though nothing had happened. When we set up for the ambush and I was soaked, mosquitos eating me up, cold despite the 80 degree temperature. Woke up the next morning still soggy and damp.

A few nights later I was in an ambush position with Joe Johnson who was a veteran rifleman in our squad from rural Georgia. He'd come over in October of 1967, four months before I arrived in early February of 1968. I guess it was around April or May and we had set up in a night ambush position outside a hooch next to a rice paddy on a wet soggy night.

There was a water buffalo tied to a wooded fence pole next to the hooch that was very aggravated by our patience. The big animals pulled plows through the rice paddies for the Vietnamese farmers in the Mekong Delta. They were everywhere. The little Vietnamese children rode atop them but they did not like American GI's.

The Vietnamese tied the animals up at night by tethering a cotton cord to a nose ring. As we sat in our positions that night around midnight the angry water buffalo broke the tethered cord and angrily headed directly toward our position. I was toting the squad's M-60 machine gun at the time. Hell, I was from LA and I didn't know anything about these animals. And when the long horned water buffalo stopped six feet from me, snorting and snarling I couldn't think of anything to do except point the machine gun at its head. I was seconds away from opening fire when Joe Johnson put his hand on my shoulder and whispered..."hold it".

With that he snapped a 7.62 mm round off the ammo belt striking it square on its noggin. As soon as it hit the beast it did a 180 and ran off into the darkness of the rice paddies. If I had shot the animal the ambush would have been busted. We would have had to get twelve guys up and moved out to some other location, set up again and lose a half night of precious sleep. As the animal ran off into the darkness Joe turned to me and whispered quietly..."that's how you handle an angry cow".

48 Home Again

My orders upon leaving Vietnam were to report at Fort Ord in Monterey, California. But first I would be granted thirty days leave to go home to Long Beach and unwind. I still owed the army six months after that to complete my two years of active duty. Our flight destination was Travis Air Force Base, California with refueling stops on Wake Island and Honolulu. From Travis we were bussed to the Oakland Army Base for processing.

After greeting my twin brother Terry and our neighbor Joe Bradford at the top of the gangway as I emerged the last passenger off the DC-9 that carried me from SFO to LAX we fetched my duffle bag at the baggage claim and walked out to the LAX parking structure. Joe Bradford drove Terry and me back from LAX to the folk's house. We took the 405 to the 91 freeway down to my home in Long Beach in Joe's hot rod fifty-five Chevy. Terry rode shot gun shotgun as I sat in the back seat, nodding off as we motored down toward North Long Beach.

It was about 9 PM on the way when we made a stop at a liquor store on the corner of Artesia Street and Cherry Avenue, a quarter mile from the folk's house, to pick up a 12 pack of Budweiser.

My Class A uniform, tie loosened, was festooned with a newly issued ribbon set and a silver and blue Combat Infantryman's Badge. Terry, Joe and I were walking around the beer cases when we saw two young women standing at the end of an aisle looking over the chilled wines. I recognized one of them right away.

Danny Powell had been head over heels for a girl named Shirley when he left for the army. He had taken her to his senior High prom but I don't think their relationship amounted to much, except in Danny's mind. But Shirley was the girl Danny had kept in is his heart when he entered the army. She was his favorite and I knew he had written to her often. I had no doubt he liked to tell his army buddies that he had a girl back home. Danny was like that.

The two of them had been classmates at Gahr High School in Artesia. Like Danny, she played a trumpet in the school band. She was Danny's buddy. They liked each other, but that was all there really was to it.

The last time I had seen her had been at Danny's funeral on the previous June 8th...eight months earlier when the army had plucked me out of battle in Vietnam's Plain of Reeds and sent me home on body escort duty to take Danny's remains home. Sure enough, the girl I recognized looking over the chilled wine there was the very same Shirley.

I didn't know what to say and when she looked up I guessed she was as surprised as me. At first I wondered if she recognized me, but a puzzled expression told me she did. After a brief awkward moment I explained the obvious. I just returned from Vietnam and I was on my way home from the airport. There was not much we could say, so as we left she just gave me a little hug and welcomed me home. She told me she was happy to see I had returned safely.

And that was it. We paid for our beers and walked out. I couldn't imagine the emotions that chance encounter might have stirred inside her and I'll never know. She knew Danny had followed me into the army and had not survived. I was safely home and Danny was gone. I never saw her again.

****

My 84 year old Grandmother, Margaret Kessler had been in Long Beach visiting my parents for a week or so. She had flown out from North Dakota had been scheduled to return home a couple days earlier, but changed her plans and stayed on to see me when she learned I was returning from home from Vietnam.

It was sweet of her and I appreciated seeing her. I had seen her last in August of 1967 when Danny and I were on our road trip before we entered the service. I know she felt badly that she had been hospitalized then, and we had only a short visit in her hospital room at the time. So there she was along with the folks and other family members and neighbor friends.

After we arrived everyone sat in living room in the folk's modest North Long Beach home sipping a few beers and chatting quietly. It was calmly overwhelming for me to be there. Safe, secure, away from the tropical heat, the sounds of gun fire, explosions and the smell of gunpowder left behind 36 hours before, excited and just beginning the process of trying to come to grips with the fact that I'd made it back, that I was actually safely home.

I had thirty days of leave before I was due to report for duty at Fort Ord on 6 March, 1969... *March 6th*... Danny Powell's birthday. He would have turned twenty on that day.

49   A Return to Fort Ord

I purchased a car when I home was on leave. It was a 1964 Opel Kadett, a boxy little blue car made by General Motors in Germany. It was a little four banger with a four speed floor shift, a hand crank sun roof and no radio. But it ran like a top. I bought it at Sal's used car lot in Bellflower. Sal was a friend of my father and he let me have it for $425. Only twenty-five bucks over what he paid for it.

On the 6th of March I drove the little Opel up Highway 101 to Fort Ord in Monterey. I had stopped at a gas station in nearby Salinas first and used a restroom to change into my requisite Class A uniform. I still owed the US Army another five months and nineteen days active duty. My orders said I was being assigned to G Company, 41st Infantry. The outfit had an acronym, CDEC.

I drove into the base and found my way to CDEC. When I checked into the Orderly Room for the first time that evening, the clerk signed me in, told me where to park the Opel and where grab a bunk for the night. I had my duffel bag with me but it contained only civilian clothes and shoes. In the morning I would be issued new olive drab colored stateside fatigues and stateside black leather army boots.

I was still in the United States Army but, truth be told, the Army had little or no use for people like me back then. But they could not, and would not let us go. Back in Vietnam any soldier who would take a voluntary tour extension until he had ninety days or less to serve in the army would be discharged upon his (or her) return. But if the Army were to release soldiers who did not take voluntary extensions there would have been no incentive to for them to extend. So even though the Army no longer had much use for 11 Bravo (Infantry) draftees back from Vietnam, they could not let us out. They were stuck with us.

So they found a warehouse for us. It was G Company, 41st Infantry at Fort Ord in USACDEC, the acronym for United States Army Combat Development Experiments Command.

I suppose CDEC, as it was commonly referred, performed some meaningful work for the military, but at Fort Ord in 1969 it was basically a holding bin for soldiers the Army needed to keep in the service for a while longer.

In our case G Company was comprised of some 150 combat infantry veterans freshly returned from tours with every infantry unit in Vietnam. We were a wild bunch of twenty through twenty-five year old young men, most of whom didn't give a damn about anything other than getting finished with the Army. Most were Specialist Fours (E-4) or (E-5) Buck Sergeants, with a sprinkling of Privates like me.

In 1969 no one, lest perhaps some psychological researchers, had any familiarity the term Post-Traumatic Stress Disorder (PTSD). As far as I know it existed in neither military nor the Veterans Administration lexicon. But I have no doubt, looking back all these years later, that most of the young men in that company at Fort Ord suffered it to one degree or another.

While on thirty day leave before reporting back to Fort Ord I had taken some time to take stock of my own mental health, and I had managed to convince myself that I was fit as a fiddle in that department. This, despite the fact I was continuously surveying all around me for places to take cover from enemy fire every time I walked around outside, flinching with shock each time I heard an sharp noise, and thinking of a place called Vietnam at least fifty times a day.

But I was not about to let Vietnam take a toll on my psyche. I had convinced myself of this since the day I had arrived there. And as soon as I would leave the military I was going to forget all about it and get on with a normal life. Back at Fort Ord now I looked upon many of my fellow soldiers at CDEC, who were mentally screwed up, with a sense of pity, arrogant and confident and self-assured they were probably not a mentally strong as I had been fortunate to be.

Many of us hoped the officers and non-commissioned officers (NCO's) in charge of us at Fort Ord would show some modicum of deference to what we had all endured and treat a fresh company of infantry combat returnees with some degree of respect. But it quickly became clear that this was not to be the case. The approach they took with us was hard line all the way. Maybe they figured we would be a difficult bunch to keep in line, and I suppose that was a real possibility.

The First Sergeant in G Company there wore a Combat Infantry Badge he'd earned in the Korean War eighteen years earlier. He had not served in Vietnam and showed little respect for us. He was an overweight E-8 that stood about 5 foot 3 inches tall with a beefy, red face and no discernible neck. Most of us took to referring to him as First Sergeant No Neck. He did not speak. He barked.

The Company Commander there was a skinny Infantry First Lieutenant who appeared to be in his early twenties who had no overseas service. He had thin blond hair, suffered from acne, and the poor guy was assigned to lord over 150 enlisted rank infantry combat returnees just back from Vietnam. To make matters worse the poor guy would likely be sent to Vietnam for his next duty assignment. And although he out ranked his charge, in our eyes he lacked the moral authority earned by combat service. His starched fatigues and polished boots mattered little to a bunch of short timer draftee combat veterans who were his charge.

The difficulties inherent in the transitioning out of combat were either ignored or misunderstood, or both, by the military as well as the individual returnees in 1969. Just about all of the returnees, myself included, had not come to terms about our circumstances. We were relieved and happy to have survived Vietnam, while at the same time we were personally coping with the loss of so many of our comrades in arms who did not return. And we all knew lots of them. The counts not only included fellow soldiers who had been killed in combat serving with us in our own units, but many more we had come to know in our training units before we were sent overseas who had been killed serving with other outfits in Vietnam.

And we were unaware of the impacts that our military service to the country was about to have on each of us for the remainder of our lives. The future trajectory of life had been altered for each one of us. We were very different people from who we were before we entered the military, and markedly different from our cohorts who had managed to avoid close quarter Vietnam combat. Most of us there believed that in a few months we would return to civilian life and quietly assimilate, storing our memories in a safe place as we would go about our lives. But the first order of business was to endure just a few easy months of stateside duty before Uncle Sam let us go.

50   Stateside Duty

On the first day back at Fort Ord I was sent over to Quartermaster Supply where I was issued three sets of fatigues, a baseball style fatigue hat, socks, underwear, a fatigue field jacket, army boots and set of olive drab colored bath towels and wash cloths.

I was assigned a bunk and an upright steel clothes locker on the second floor of one of the old style wooden barracks structures that were then common to lower Fort Ord. Diagonal parking spaces were provided on the company street out front.

When I returned with my newly issued clothing around mid-morning I changed into fatigues, made my way down to the company street and ascended the short flight of stairs to the landing outside in front of the Orderly Room door, walked in and reported.

I was wearing no rank insignia yet, no unit patch or name tag. We were required to purchase for ourselves at the Post Exchange and have them stitched on at the Fort Ord Post tailor. The army provided us with expense reimbursement after we had purchased the patches had them sewn, but it took a couple days to get this done. Hence, new arrivals were easily recognized.

The NCO working the Orderly Room checked me in. As he did so he raised an eyebrow my way as he was taking note on his clip board that I was an E-3 Private First Class (PFC). Returning from Vietnam holding any rank south of E-4 immediately labeled one as screw-up. So with dispatch he sent me out on a work detail at a battalion chaplain's office a couple blocks away.

I walked over to the Chaplain's office and reported to the chaplain's assistant, a young Specialist Four (E-4). I didn't really know how these guys came to be assigned to that kind of duty, but I figured they must have been plugged into their assignments by pre-arrangements when they joined the army. The army was just like any other large government bureaucracy, and they could get special people assigned to certain jobs through family connections. At any rate I figured this kid was pretty lucky to be assigned where he was in March of 1969.

He was a nice young chap and he put a mop in my hand and had me cleaning the floors of the chaplain's quarters, later dusting shelves, and sweeping porches. I said nothing to him as I quietly went about my work until finally, taking an afternoon break.

During the break we struck up a conversation where he asked me where I was from, and how long I had been in the army. I explained to him that I was from down in Long Beach, and I had just arrived at Fort Ord following a thirty day leave after completing my tour in Vietnam.

He looked surprised and I guess he felt guilty. He told me that he thought I was a new recruit on my second day in the army before heading up the hill for basic training. And then he took the broom away from me and told me to take the rest of the day off and he finished the sweeping himself.

It was kind of funny because I had enjoyed working there all day without getting shot at.

51 Witt

The last time I had seen Ron Witt he had been standing outside of a mess hall at the Oakland Army Base smoking a cigarette a couple days before we each boarded jet planes bound for Vietnam, more than a year before. Covered with baking flour, he was on KP duty taking a smoke break.

Witt was a young man from Bellflower, California, the city next to Paramount, where I grew up. He was a couple years older than me, and in Bellflower he had lived just a few houses away from my own childhood best friend, Dennis Cable when Dennis' family resided there before moving to Paramount.

Dennis had known both Ron and Ron's younger brother, Chuckie, from his old neighborhood. Ron Witt had been a Bellflower "low rider" kind of car club guy when he was in high school. He had driven a big Chevy that he cruised Bellflower Boulevard, often smoking dope with his car club friends during his high school years.

Four years after high school he found himself in the army because a municipal judge offered to excuse some legal malfeasance on his part if Mr. Witt would follow his just recently received US Army induction orders.

So he was drafted and, like me, he ended up at Fort Polk's Tigerland for infantry training following his basic training. We met and became acquainted there and became buddies often hanging out together.

On one cold November, 1967 morning there we were to be trained in the use of the Starlight Scope night vision device. But just before the block of instruction was set to begin Ron was called out from the company and told he was prohibited from attending the training. The Starlight Scope was a secret classified army thing back then, and because Ron Witt had a minor criminal record he was prohibited from attending the one hour block of instruction about the Starlight Scope.

So the army was sending Ron Witt to Vietnam as an infantryman where he would probably be using the Starlight Scope damn near every night he was in the field, but he was prohibited in attending the training class on how to use it because it was a some sort of secret equipment and, due to Witt's petty criminal infraction history, he lacked the clearance to take the class.

It was one of those classes where the army trained us for a full hour that the way to use the Starlight Scope was to turn on the toggle switch atop the device, look through the end of it and focus it.

It didn't matter that he missed the instruction. After the class I filled Witt in on the Starlight Scope. My lesson took three five minutes, including time for questions. We both thought it was cool that at least we would be able see the bad guys over there in Vietnam in the dark.

As previously stated, my last image of Ron Witt was of a young man, slight of build, covered in baking flour in back of a mess hall smoking a cigarette at the Oakland Army base in February of 1968. But just a few months after that, when I was in Vietnam I heard through the grapevine Ron Witt had been killed in action serving with the Fourth Infantry Division in the Central Highlands of Vietnam.

So it came as a shock when I walked out of the Fort Ord Post Exchange (PX) annex a couple days after reporting to Fort Ord when I practically bumped into Ronnie Witt walking out as he was walking in.

"Jesus Christ Witt. You're supposed to be dead", I said.

Like me, Witt had just reported to Fort Ord. And it turned out he too was to be assigned to CDEC, G Company 41st Infantry. We were to be in the same company.

We embraced and shook hands with a laugh. Witt's laugh was a soft "eh", "eh", "eh". Maybe a fourth "eh" if he was really cracking up at something. I told him I heard he'd been killed in a firefight several months back with the Fourth Division. He expressed surprise at that and explained he had taken an AK-47 round in his shoulder during a fire fight, then he'd been medevac'd out and flown to a field hospital and then on to a hospital in Japan for surgery and recuperation for some months.

It was not uncommon for comrades to believe somebody was dead when dusted out. Men see someone down and bleeding, being treated by a frantic field medic and assume the worst. The rumors start. Then you run into someone you knew from training at an enlisted men's (EM) club somewhere and word spreads.

Witt unbuttoned his fatigue shirt and showed me a large, impressive scar running around his shoulder, a result of his wound. So I told him how I'd got shot in the face in Vietnam but only had two stiches and went back to field duty after just one day.

Witt was one of those characters you figured most likely to be tossed out of the army with a bad conduct discharge at some point. He quietly disobeyed more orders, missed or arrived late for more duty calls for guard duty or KP, and generally thumbed his nose at military authority more than anyone I ever met in the army. But here he was. Alive and well with the same shit eating grin he always wore. Back from Vietnam like me. And he had been busted in rank so many times that he was just a Private E-2. The second lowest rank in the US military. And he was probably the only guy in our new company I outranked.

It was good seeing him alive and well and I cheerfully scratched his name off the *list of the* dead I was carrying around in my brain.

52 Hunter Liggett

Fort Ord smelled good. The Monterey Bay area had a nice fragrance that was a mix of Eucalyptus and fresh ocean air. If I still owed the army time I was happy it would be here. But I soon discovered that Fort Ord was mostly to be a staging post for CDEC troops.

When I arrived at CDEC I had not the foggiest notion what they did, and why they posted a bunch of infantry guys in a combat weapons research and development operation. But I soon found out we were to be used to test out some of the new army toys under development by Litton Industries, a Pentagon military contractor, for what were mostly remotely monitored ground troop detection sensors.

To do this work the army would load us into the backs of several deuce and a half trucks to haul us south to the Hunter Liggett Military Reservation located in the most geographically isolated part of the State of California.

To get there we were convoyed out through Salinas, eighty-six miles down Highway 101 to a point just north of the King City, then southwest over twenty-five miles of two lane winding road.

In 1969 the Hunter Liggett Military Reservation consisted of a dozen or so World War II vintage Quonset hut barracks, a small post exchange and a little snack bar that served beer, sodas, burgers, fries and hot dogs. It covered a couple hundred square miles of oak studded rolling hills and trails.

Our job there took us down from Fort Ord on Mondays. On Tuesdays, Wednesdays and Thursdays we were trucked out into the hills each morning, dumped out of deuce and a half's and ordered to tromp over the mountain trails all day.

The Litton Industries' plastic camouflaged motion and vibration detectors had been planted along the trails. As we dutifully trooped past them they were remotely monitored by technicians.

That was pretty much the lot of the returning combat infantryman sent to Hunter Liggett. Five or six months of hot, sweaty and boring duty while we waited to finish our two years of military service. Not exactly rocket science.

Arriving back at Hunter Liggett proper each evening after a day of tromping over the hills we showered and went to company formation where First Sergeant No Neck would bark at us for about ten minutes. When formation broke we could hit the tiny snack bar to buy a burger and a six-pack of beer for dinner.

On Friday mornings we were trucked back out State Highway 33 to US 101 up through Salinas and back to Fort Ord. Around four in the afternoon we were usually released for the weekend to be due back by 6 AM revelry on Monday morning to do it all again.

Not surprisingly, drugs were everywhere in G Company. On weekends when First Lieutenant Pimples and First Sergeant No Neck left the base, marijuana, amphetamines, barbiturates, LSD and God knows what else, were sold, traded and consumed openly.

To make matters worse, we quickly picked up on the fact that we were being demonized as baby killers by many of our civilian cohorts. Most, of us were struggling to adjust to our personal post-Vietnam War lives. And as young soldiers off the base we were conspicuous in appearance with close cropped hair and clean shaved faces while other young men of the era of wore long hair, sloppy beards and mustaches as they marched over college campuses protesting the war. It was an activity that included denigrating and ostracizing war weary returning draftees in a colossal and disgraceful display of national ignorance. Eighteen months earlier during the *Summer of Love* most of us had been taking bayonet training in basic training. We were different, and it left many soldiers confused, angry, and bewildered.

The military offered about one hour of counseling about transitioning back into the civilian world on the day before you were to be set free, but nothing along those lines while serving out the remaining five or six months still owed the army.

We were directed to change into civilian attire when we left base on leave and to avoid conflict with the locals in the Monterey area, and we were ordered to completely stay out of King City, the closest town to the Hunter Liggett Military Reservation. King City was off limits. But no one really much cared. All of us wanted just one thing above all else: Out of the army and a return to civilian life, where we naively believed we would be able to quickly put our individual memories of the previous two years behind us.

With every new duty assignment in the military we had been integrated into a company of strangers. New people with much in common. Wearing an army uniform is like wearing a book describing your military life. The patch on your left shoulder identified the unit to which you were assigned. A combat patch on the right shoulder signified the unit you served with in combat. No right shoulder patch means you had not served in a combat zone.

The uniform shows your rank, your military occupation and each ribbon on a Class "A" uniform represents a medal or unit citation. Badges above the ribbons represented infantry combat service or completion of airborne jump school. People in the army can tell a whole lot about other soldiers in a couple seconds just by looking at the uniform.

At G Company at Fort Ord every infantry unit in Vietnam was represented. We knew if a guy had served in the Central Highlands (4th Infantry Division), Cu Chi (25th Infantry Division), Lai Kai (1st Infantry Division), and on and on. They were all there. 101st Airborne, 82nd Airborne, 196th LIB, 198th LIB, 199 LIB, 11th Armored Cav, other guys from the 9th Infantry Division too, and all the rest of them. We'd all gone to Vietnam as infantry grunts and we all came home from that war with the same different experiences. We were happy to be alive, looking forward to release from the military, and marking time with no greater sense of purpose beyond military service separation.

53 Military Minimum Wage

The army held pay day at the end of each month. Stateside pay for an E-4 Specialist Four was around $195 a month back then, and only around $140 for an E-3 PFC. Since I had been busted from E-4 to E-3 while back in Vietnam with orders making my lower rank retroactive for more than six months it became painfully obvious that I would not have happy pay days at Fort Ord.

Since the orders making me a Private First Class for the second time in my military career were processed in December back in Vietnam and made effective from the previous July, the army now claimed it had been "overpaying" me at the E-4 rate for about six months.

And the army wanted its money back. So arriving at Fort Ord in March of 1969 after surviving my twelve months of Vietnam service I owed the US Army about five or six hundred dollars in back pay. As a consequence my monthly pay for the next five or six months would be the grand sum of ten bucks. Talk about your minimum wage...I was working for ten bucks a month. It was called "health and comfort" pay.

Coming home many of us expected to be greeted with respect by our fellow Americans. Regardless how one felt about the war we were veterans who had given our country our blood, sweat and tears and we had served with honor. But we quickly discovered that we were badly misinformed. Instead of respect we were treated by many of our fellow countrymen as baby killers, and war criminal losers. And it seemed that there were elements of the army establishment that felt the same way about us.

Over the course of our army service we had trained among strangers starting back in basic training. We trained again in advanced infantry training units among new strangers. We were then sent out to dozens of different military units into combat in Vietnam among strangers. And finally we were sent home to stateside units to complete our military obligation to with another unit of strangers. By the time we came back to Fort Ord following Vietnam most of us were tired of making new friends and by this time the overwhelming majority of us just wanted to get out of the army.

So we didn't forge a lot of new friendships this time around. Most of the guys there were marching to their own drummers by then with feet in the army and minds out of it. We were friendly and there were casual friendships. But it seemed as if everyone was busy dealing with their own experiences from Vietnam. Everyone was from a different unit, a different company, a different platoon in Vietnam, and each young man had his own different, unique combat experiences. No one was particularly interested in sharing war stories either. Everyone was just trying to forget about it, to be out of the army, and to be free again.

The army had its own ideas. Morning formation was at six AM Monday through Friday. And First Sergeant No Neck consistently displayed his deep seeded resentment for what he considered a bunch of dope smoking draftees with no greater desire other than get out of his beloved army.

The United States Army was just beginning to suffer the hangover from the war in Vietnam while there were still more than 500,000 troops over there. President Richard Nixon's presidency was just beginning and the Paris Peace talks were going nowhere fast. Losing the war was taking a toll and nowhere did it seem more evident than G Company at Fort Ord, a holding tank for a bunch of worn out young infantry vets trying to come to grips with where they had been, what they had been through, and where they were going.

First Lieutenant Pimples was the warden and First Sergeant No Neck was the head guard. It seemed as if neither one of them wanted to be there any more than the inmates serving out the last months of a two year sentence in the army. So the young vets there obeyed the rules, without individual initiatives, each waiting for the day to be presented with that big white envelope that contained army separation papers.

54   Base Wanderings

General Omar Bradley was one of the very rare five star generals in the United States Army ever so promoted. A famous and highly distinguished World War II command general, he had retired from active duty in 1953. In 1945 through 1948 he served as head of the Department of Veterans Affairs as Army Chief of Staff, and later as Chairman of the Joint Chiefs of Staff for two terms during the Korean War.

On one weekend sometime in the spring of 1969 the retired General Bradley paid a visit to Fort Ord. I do not remember what the occasion was, or if it was even some sort of special occasion for that matter. I can only recall that all our weekend leaves were cancelled so we could don Class A uniforms to march in formation past the general as he stood on a reviewing stand there. Afterward we listened to a couple of tributes to the general given by the top brass at Fort Ord.

I didn't know exactly who he was at the time, only that I had heard of his name and knew he was a famous World War II general. It was all over by early afternoon on the Saturday or Sunday that it was held.

There were more than a few weekends that I stayed on at Ord over the weekend even if I had leave. It was economics. Because I was earning a whopping ten bucks a month it didn't leave much spending money for gas and burgers, and there were always open mess halls open on base where I could eat or free on weekends.

On these weekends I found I could walk into any enlisted men's mess hall on the base wearing my fatigues at any meal time and get into the chow line. Nobody ever cared who I was. After a while I found where the better ones were. The base hospital's mess hall was a good one, and the chow there did not taste bad to me, especially given that I had just spent the better part of an entire year eating C Rations for almost every meal in Vietnam.

On the weekends when I did drive down to Long Beach I gave rides to other soldiers in return for gas money. Ron Witt was one of the guys who rode down and back there with me many times. We would head out for LA around four on Friday afternoon and make it down to LA by ten that night. When Sunday night rolled around we would head back up to Fort Ord around ten PM and stumble back in around 4 AM. We were young and strong enough to get through Monday on a couple hours of sleep.

On many weekend afternoons I'd have some beers and walk around Ord. One of those afternoons I wandered up to where the basic combat training barracks were located. My mind took me back to seventeen months earlier when I was going through basic there. It seemed like such a long time had passed, and it felt weird when a drill instructor or some other NCO would walk past as I was strolling around and I would not to be verbally assaulted and dressed down. They could see by the patch and Combat Infantryman's Badge embroidered on my fatigues that I was not one of their trainees, but just another fellow soldier on base. Of course passing by an officer there required a salute and one returned. I took to taking walks around the base often to kill time on many of weekends I spent there.

On one afternoon I happened upon an outdoor assembly area next to a base chapel where there looked to be sixty of seventy civilians congregated. Some kind of ceremony was going on, and I quietly walked up behind the assemblage to see what was going on. I was a couple hundred feet back so I stopped for a few minutes to listen to the speaker who was addressing the group.

I soon realized it was a memorial service for a soldier who had fallen in Vietnam. The people there were his family members and friends, and they were formally dressed and reverent. So out of curiosity I stood there quietly, out of sight under a tree and listened to the speaker. Then he spoke the name of the fallen soldier.

It turned out the service was for a young man from San Jose, California. And it was for John Mc Gehee who had been killed serving in my very same platoon back in Vietnam. I was astonished standing back there that afternoon at Fort Ord witnessing that service.

I wondered if I should approach Mc Gehee's family as the service was breaking up to introduce myself. But I would not know what to say to them. Maybe they would ask me questions about John's duties and how he died and I would find myself unable to even talk about him. I had only know him for a couple weeks there and then he was gone. And I was wearing wrinkled fatigues smelling of cigarettes and beer and I was twenty years of age. I just walked away.

Of all the military bases in the United States, how was it that I had stumbled across a memorial service for a fallen soldier from my own squad in Vietnam?

55 An Official Reprimand

At one point in the spring of 1969 the Secretary of the Army in Washington D.C. issued a directive regarding mustaches. For those who were not born or old enough to remember that time let it just be said that every twenty-something young man in America wanted to sport a mustache, if not more facial hair. Facial hair was a symbol of rebellious manhood in those days. The amount of hair, be it long, stringy, greasy locks and/or a mustache and beard, a guy sported was directly related to his rebellious manhood.

So it was no surprise that the first order of business for nearly every young man getting out of the military was to begin growing that mustache. When the Secretary of the Army issued the mustache directive permitting soldiers to wear modest, well-trimmed mustaches the word spread like wildfire. Almost every member of G Company showed up to the following Monday morning formation at Hunter Liggett sporting three days growth of mustache.

And it took First Sergeant No Neck about one minute to inform the troopers standing in formation that morning that he did not care what the directive issued by the Secretary of the Army said. Every member of G Company was to be "slick lipped", as he put it, by formation the following morning. And so it would be.

On a weekend shortly thereafter Ron Witt and I went down to LA for the weekend. As was our custom I dropped him off at his mother's house in Bellflower Friday night before heading on to Long Beach. And as was also our custom I picked him up about 10 PM on Sunday night for the drive north back to Fort Ord. We both signed in at the G Company orderly room around 4 AM on Monday morning, made the 6AM morning formation to begin another week of duty with CDEC.

A couple weeks after one of those weekend trips to LA I was ordered to report to the office of our Company Commander, First Lieutenant Pimples. So what was this all about? I was not prone to creating any problems at Fort Ord as I awaited the day that was very soon to come when I was to be honorably separated from the US Army.

So I was surprised that when I reported, First Lieutenant Pimples ordered me to attention before his desk and read out a Uniform Code of Military Justice Article 15 charging me with having failed to report for guard duty some two weeks earlier. This was news to me since I had no knowledge of having been ordered to perform guard duty on the date specified.

I asked First Lieutenant Pimples to show me the supposedly posted order that I had not seen. He refused. Told me it had been posted. Told me to sign the Article 15, which meant I could be busted in rank or fined.

I had signed one of those before back in Vietnam when Major Loefke busted me from Specialist Four to PFC and fined me $60.00. This time I was not inclined to do the same. So I told First Lieutenant Pimples that I wished to speak to legal counsel at the Judge Advocate General's (JAG) Office at Fort Ord before deciding what to do.

First Lieutenant Pimples allowed then grudgingly me to visit said office and return in a couple hours to settle the matter. So I walked over to the JAG's office. I went in and asked to speak with a military attorney. A Sergeant First Class at the office there told me there were no lawyers around at the time. So I explained the situation to the Sergeant and asked for his opinion.

He told me he was not an attorney and he could not advise me. Then, when I was casually walking away, I asked him what he would do if he was me. He just shook his head and said, "Hell, I wouldn't sign anything."

So I returned to First Lieutenant Pimples' office, stood before him at his desk, and told him that I was innocent of the charge and I would not agree to and sign the Article 15. The alternative to an Article 15 was trial by general court martial. But I was pretty sure that First Lieutenant Pimples was not about to make a federal case about this and I had called his bluff.

He rocked back in his chair for a moment then ordered me to stand at attention. Then he stood up behind his desk and said he was going to give me a verbal reprimand in lieu of a court martial. Standing at attention before him I said, "Okay." He then told me I was "hereby reprimanded".

We saluted each other and I did an about face and exited his office. That was the end of that matter.

Lieutenant Pimples was really not such a bad guy, but he was pretty typical of the attitude toward draftees returned from their tours in Vietnam. Today it's common knowledge that the civilian treatment veterans received in those days was a national disgrace, but sadly and lesser known is the fact that the treatment many returnees received finishing up their enlistments stateside after serving tours in Vietnam from the US Army itself was not much different.

56 On Light Duty

In early May of 1969 with less than two months to go before my release from the army I was riding in the back of an open deuce and a half through the hills of the Hunter Liggett Military Reservation one morning when my army baseball cap blew off as we were hauled out to tramp around in the hills for the day. Several hours later as we headed back in toward the Quonset hut barracks the driver spotted the cap lying along the side of the road.

He pulled over to the road side and stopped so I could retrieve it. As I was hopping out the back over the vehicle's tail gate it gave way. Whoever closed it had failed to latch it properly. It moved downward about six inches from my weight before the chain stopped the gate preventing it from falling completely open. But it fell open enough to cause me to lose my grip on the top of the tailgate and fall to the asphalt pavement five feet below.

I landed in a prone position with my left elbows and knees taking the brunt of the fall. Both knees were cut and bruised and my left elbow was cut and bruised as well. The company field medic came over and provided first aid and small bandages. With the hat in tote I climbed up into the back of the truck and rode back to the barracks to spend the night.

By next morning the elbow was throbbing and too stiff to do much bending so I was instructed to hop a resupply truck ride back up to Fort Ord to have the arm x-rayed.

That afternoon I visited the Fort Ord medical facility. I received the x-ray and was told to come back in an hour to see a doctor and get the results. It was lunch time so I popped into the mess hall cafeteria there and got a tray with a burger and potato chips.

As I was sitting down for lunch there I felt a tap on the shoulder behind me. I turned my head back and looked up to see none other than Clarke (Doc) Scherff, our third platoon medic from Charlie Company, 2nd of the 60th Infantry in Vietnam, and the very same medic who had treated me in the field there when I had been wounded the previous March. Doc had himself later been medevac'd out and back to the states after he was badly wounded in a fire fight in June of 1968. I hadn't seen him since June 1st of that year, about ten months before.

I guessed that Doc Scherff was recovering from his wounds and working at the Fort Ord Medical Hospital. It was quite a happy surprise to run into him there. I told him the reason I was there that day and we caught up on events over lunch. He was eager to learn about the guys in the third platoon he left behind there and I shared as much as I could about the guys who survived and some sad news of some that didn't. But it was fabulous to see him again.

After lunch in the examination room the doctor posted my x-ray over fluorescent light hanging on the wall and shared the results with me. It showed there was a small bone crack on the tip of the left elbow. The doctor told me I would need to keep the arm in a sling to keep it stable but that placing the arm in a caste would not do any good. It would take five or six weeks to heal.

Now, by this time I only had about six more weeks before I was to be discharged from the army, and with an arm in a sling I would have to be placed on some sort of light duty. It was a certainty that my infantry duty days were now over.

Light duty orders were referred to as being placed on "profile". The doctor would fill out and sign a "profile" order that contained a check list of activities that were not to be performed.

So when the doctor sat down and began checking off the activities I would not be allowed to perform for the next six weeks I spoke up and, half kidding, asked him to write me up a good one because I only had six weeks to go.

Now, the army drafted most of its medical doctors for a couple of years in those days and they were routinely assigned the rank of captain. But most considered themselves to be civilians in uniforms. So when I told him I had just six weeks left the doctor glanced up at me over his clip board laughing and said, "Why you sonofabitch. I've got *seven* weeks to go!"

He then proceeded to check off just about every item on the profile order list, including one that said "No Prolonged Standing". Then he signed it and handed me the profile form to present to my First Sergeant along with a copy for me, wished me well, and sent me on my way.

When I returned to G Company that afternoon I saw First Sergeant No Neck in the Orderly Room and gave him his copy of the profile order. He looked at it and read the list of banned activities. Then he muttered a few profanities and told me he wanted to see me every morning at the company formation. After the morning formation broke he did not want to see my face again until the next morning's formation.

So I was to spend the final six weeks before leaving the army on my own except for making the morning formation on Monday through Friday. That was it. That was the only duty I was to perform until the day I was to leave the military. I did not even have to make my bunk. Just jam the sheets, blanket and pillow into my metal locker each morning and leave the bunk with a bare mattress.

So I taped a copy of my profile order on the inside door of my locker and anytime some superior would order me to do anything I would show him the order. And that would be the end of it. It was like gold.

57 Carmel by the Sea

With no duties to perform I needed to figure out what to do with myself. My two year enlistment was originally scheduled to be completed on 25 August 1969, but it had been extended to 31 August in order for me to pay back the military the six days the army said I owed it for having been A.W.O.L. in June of 1968 when I was returning to my unit in Vietnam from escorting Danny Powell's remains for burial in Southern California.

But I learned that I could get an "early out" of up to ninety days to start college classes. So I applied to and was accepted at Cerritos Junior College in Norwalk, California for the summer session that was to begin in mid-June. After turning in the paper work I was given the upcoming date of 11 June for my release from active duty. I told Ron Witt about it so he also jumped on it and applied for college at Cerritos JC and was given the same active duty separation date.

So with six weeks left I began to spend most of my days down at the beach at Carmel, a few miles south of Fort Ord. I would stand at morning duty formation Monday through Friday, a task that typically took about five or ten minutes as First Lieutenant Pimples or First Sergeant No Neck, or some underling would announce the daily orders.

When the formation broke I would head out in my Opel down to Carmel following breakfast at the company mess hall and a change of clothes from my army fatigues to civvies.

I would spend the early part of each day hiking around the town sight-seeing then after lunch I would usually use my limited funds to purchase a jug of Gallo Red Mountain wine that I would take out to the beach where I would sip the vino from a paper cup, smoke cigarettes, do a little reading and contemplate my world. I found that I pretty much liked the daily solitude and getting half blasted there each afternoon.

A couple weeks into this routine I was called in to the Orderly Room by a sergeant following the morning formation. He told me First Sergeant No Neck wanted to see me. So before heading over to the mess hall for breakfast I hiked up the front steps to the Orderly Room counter. Inside the First Sergeant was standing about ten feet behind the counter when I reported in. He didn't say anything at first. Instead he was glaring at me as he was wadding a sheet of paper into a ball. Then he wound up and threw it at me so fast that it bounced off my chest.

As I bent down for it picking it up from the floor the First Sergeant said "This is for you, Brooks. Now get out of here!"

So I walked quietly down the stairs and out to the company street where I opened up the wadded sheet.

It was an order list for award of the Good Conduct Medal. Half way down the list of names on the orders I found my name highlighted. I was thusly awarded a United States Army Good Conduct Medal, and I had a sneaky suspicion that the good First Sergeant was none too happy to see me so decorated.

The month of June finally arrived and I was to spend the final days of my military service hanging out at Carmel's public beach looking out over the Pacific Ocean. I thought a lot about a lot of things out there. Mostly about the previous twenty-two months I'd spent in the army.

I had arrived at Fort Ord's Reception Station just a week shy of my nineteenth birthday and now I was about a week and a half away from completing my active duty military commitment, once again at Fort Ord, at the ripe old age of twenty. I had come full circle.

One afternoon I found myself thinking about a day back when I was in basic training at Fort Ord. There was a short skinny kid named Perry. Perry was his last name, of course, because it seemed nobody in the army had a first name. Your last name was sewn on to your fatigue shirt above the pocket so that was how everybody knew everyone else.

Anyway, Perry was a kid that liked to chew gum. But chewing gum while standing in company formation was not allowed. Perry had been caught chewing gum a couple of times. Punishment was taking the gum out of your mouth and sticking it to the end of your nose, and that is exactly how Perry had been so punished, leaving it there for a couple hours until given permission to remove it.

One morning as the company stood in formation in the company street waiting for the company commander, a young captain, to descend the stairs from his office behind the Orderly Room Perry stood in the front row once again chewing gum. A drill corporal spotted him chewing away. This drill corporal was pretty much a bad ass type who loved intimidating young basic trainees. He wore heavily starched fatigues and he liked to put his face about two inches away from your nose as he screamed and berated you.

True to form he stood face to face with Perry and was practically spitting in his face asking Perry if he was chewing gum. "Yes drill corporal", Perry yelled. Knowing that Perry knew the drill, the drill corporal, his face two inches from Perry's nose, pointed an index finger at his own nose and told Perry, "Right here Private Perry"!

That's when Perry calmly took the wad of gum from his mouth and in one quick motion stuck it right on the tip of the corporal's nose.

For a split second I thought the drill corporal's beet red head was going to explode. But just as this was happening the captain was walking down the steps and he had witnessed the entire episode. He wisely intervened between Perry and the drill corporal, who by this time had brushed the gum from his nose. The captain then ordered Perry to police up the gum and to take a lap around the barracks as punishment, as he tried vainly to conceal his own laughter.

The episode probably raised the spirits of the trainees in that basic training company more than anything else during the entire eight weeks we spent there. And Perry became the hero of every trainee in the company.

Upon completion of that basic training cycle at least ninety-five percent of the draftees in that company were ordered to be trained as light weapons infantrymen. And ninety-five percent of those had subsequently been sent off to fight in the jungles and rice paddies of Vietnam.

Nearly all of them had remained at Fort Ord for infantry training, but I was one of a small handful sent to Fort Polk, Louisiana for advanced infantry training (AIT) from where every graduate was sent to Vietnam upon completion of training. In the end it wasn't much different for the guys who remained at Fort Ord. Ninety percent of them went to Vietnam as well.

After basic training I lost track of nearly everyone in that basic combat training company. It has been called the *Summer of Love* in San Francisco, but sadly, I have no doubt that a great many of the draftees who cycled through basic training in the fall of 1967 never made it home from Vietnam.

Eighteen months later I sat on the beach at Carmel by the Sea thinking about the Mekong Delta, some 12,000 miles across the Pacific Ocean. I still had buddies there and I hoped they would all complete their twelve month tours safely. My feet were in California but my mind was still very much over there as I looked westward over the waters.

58 Chewed Up and Spit Out

On weekend trips down to Long Beach I would don civilian clothes and pretend to be a civilian. For two days I could imagine what it was going to be like when I was out of the army. I imagined myself a young guy in college going to parties, meeting good looking girls, planning and preparing for a life where I would get a great job, marry a pretty girl, have a couple of kids and live the American Dream.

There was something going on that was hard to figure though. I had been army for less than two years but I discovered there was a profound difference among people my age between the ones that stayed home and the ones who had gone off to the war. It was a difference that was not based on any kind of overt hostility that I personally experienced, but with some people it felt like there was a curious animosity going on. It was hard to figure because regardless how people felt about Vietnam it seemed incomprehensible that some people could hold a kid drafted to fight there responsible. But I soon learned that that was exactly what was going on.

And the days dwindled down to *the day*. On the tenth of June with one more day to go I was called to the Orderly Room following the morning formation. The First Sergeant had an order in his hand for me to report to the Fort Ord motor pool to test for an army driver's license.

In the army a soldier needed a special army driver's license to pilot army jeeps and trucks. I reminded my First Sergeant that I already had orders in hand to be discharged the next day, and it seemed like it would be a waste of time for me to obtain an army driver's license that I would never use. He didn't care. I think he just wrote out the order himself to get rid of me for the day knowing that I would be permanently gone the following day.

I never really personally gave First Sergeant No Neck any grief. But he knew I that I was a wise ass PFC who had refused to sign First Lieutenant Pimples' Article 15, that I had a medical profile that kept me from performing any and all duties, that I had never spit shined a pair of boots in my entire almost two year military career, and that I showed up every morning at the company formation wearing wrinkled fatigues I had yanked out and donned right out of the latrine clothes dryer.

I suppose for him I was a pretty easy read. So the day before I got out of the army I obediently headed over to the motor pool to take the test to obtain an army driver's license. I took and passed the written test. Then I was given a depth perception exam that I failed miserably. So I washed out. But I did the old First Sergeant a favor and kept out of his sight for the rest of the day.

On the eleventh of June, 1969 I woke up, showered, shaved, packed up my duffel bag and dressed in my Class A uniform. My friend Private Ron Witt did the same. That morning the two of us signed out of G Company and reported to the processing center at Fort Ord to get discharged from active duty.

Along with dozens of other young men we were given cursory physical exams after which we went to an office where a dozen or so army clerks were typing away on DD 214 forms, the official separation orders.

The DD 214 form contains an official summary of your military records. Among other things it denotes the character of your service (Honorable), rank (E-3), military specialty (11B-10, Light Weapons Infantry) and awards and decorations. When your DD 214 was ready you were called to the counter and handed a pen to sign it.

Then with a bunch of other papers and a couple hundred dollars separation pay it was placed in a large white envelope with an official records logo printed on the outside.

The magic moment arrived when you were handed that envelop. With that you were free to leave the military. All that was left was to get in your car and drive away to freedom. Never to return.

I made it through the process a few minutes before Ron Witt. I was giving him a lift down to LA so I waited for him outside the processing center holding my big white envelope that contained my separation orders. About ten minutes later Witt caught up with me outside carrying the same large white envelope with his own separation papers.

We wasted no time heading over to the G Company Street where my little Opel was parked and waiting. But one more little incident happened along the way. We were wearing our Class "A" uniforms as we passed within about thirty feet of an army major who was walking in the opposite direction. We both kind of glanced off in the opposite direction since we were in that gray area where a salute is required or maybe not. But he obviously took note of the big white official records envelopes that a couple of privates were each carrying. In other words he knew we were about ten minutes from leaving Fort Ord and the United States Army forever.

He promptly walked stridently in our direction where he confronted us and chewed us out for failing to salute him. We both apologized, stood at attention and saluted him. Then, glaring at us, he allowed us to go on our way.

We had been told that you are technically still members of the active military for seventy-two more hours after you get your separation papers and it was not a time to try being wise asses.

We finally made it to my car and headed toward the Salinas gate out of Fort Ord. We both felt a sense of anticipation as we approached the unmanned exit. Hell, I had dreamed of this moment for nearly two years. But as we motored past the gate Witt suddenly cried out for me to stop the car! I slowed down to pull over as Witt grabbed his door handle and started to exit the vehicle. I grabbed his arm and asked him what the hell he was doing. The area there was devoid of anything man made except for the Fort Ord chain link fence and barbed wire. Then Witt told me he wanted to get out and defecate (not his exact words) on the road right outside the gate, but I pulled him back into the car and we rolled away before he had time to argue. He had actually wanted to tell the army goodbye by taking a dump on the road. Such was his final opinion of the United States Army.

For my part I began to feel a strange and unexpected sense of loss as we passed through that gate. I guess I realized that the army had been serving as a platform for me to deposit my anger, which was something I dearly needed. Now it was gone and I was going to have to figure out a new way to deal with whatever was inside that I needed to expel. I had survived Vietnam and I made it through the rest of the time I owed the Army. But I realized that in the span of one year nine and a half months both Ron Witt and I, like thousands of other young vets, had been pretty much chewed up and spit out.

Before hitting the freeway we stopped at a liquor store in Salinas where Witt asked me to pick up a couple of Dixie cups with ice and straws at a burger place across the street as he went into the store. When I came back to the car Witt was already there sitting in his passenger seat twisting the cap off a jug of Gallo Red Mountain burgundy that was discreetly sitting down on the floor in front of him.

Postscript

Some thirty years after my discharge a military review board conducted an examination of the daily unit logs of the 2nd of the 60th Infantry for the date I had been wounded in Vietnam and awarded me the Purple Heart Medal and had my military separation records corrected. The accompanying Purple Heart certificate was officially signed and dated on September 4th, 1998... the occasion of my fiftieth birthday. The medal along with several other decorations were conveyed to me a couple months thereafter via US Mail.

An exhaustive, historical account of the 2nd Battalion, 60th Infantry of the 9th Infantry Division in Vietnam is entitled In the Land of Nine Dragons: The 2nd Battalion, 60th Infantry in Southeast Asia, 1966-1970. This voluminous work is a comprehensive account of the unit compiled by former soldier scholars who fought on the ground there. It provided details and accounts of life in the unit that cannot be remotely approached in a simple memoir based on personal recollections of events forty years ago by one former soldier.

The statistical research contained in *Nine Dragons* found that during its forty-five months of deployment to Vietnam and Cambodia at least 348 soldiers lost their lives serving with the 2nd Battalion, 60th Infantry, and more than 1,687 were awarded Purple Hearts serving with the unit there. The battalion along with the rest of the First Brigade of the Ninth Infantry Division was awarded the Presidential Unit Citation by President Lyndon Johnson for conspicuous sustained gallantry for a period of combat that began in June of 1968.

The Coffelt Data Base is an exhaustive, privately developed compilation of casualty statistics for individual military units in Vietnam. It contains the names of individuals who died in Vietnam by date of casualty, by cause of death where available, and by unit assignment down to the company level for the United States Army; and other branches of the U. S. military, in addition to other factors such as home town and more. It provided me with information and details of the twenty-eight soldiers I served with in Charlie Company who were killed during the twelve month period of my own tour of duty there.

Three days after I was separated from the army on June 14th, 1969 President Richard Nixon ordered the redeployment of the Ninth Infantry Division out of Vietnam. It was the very first American division withdrawn from Vietnam by the President as part of the American drawdown of forces from the war.

About a month later in July of 1969 Neil Armstrong set foot on the moon and I watched the historical moon landing on television while sitting on a bar stool at Clem's Starlight Lounge in Paramount, California while sipping a beer on my fake I.D.

In the years immediately following I witnessed the Vietnam protest era along with the rest of my generation by sequestering myself first in Junior College and then in State College in California and moving to Northern California to escape the smog and freeways of Southern California in 1972.

Shortly after leaving the army I lost contact with Ron Witt. The next twenty-seven years were spent making a living while pretending to forget the twenty-one and one half months I spent in the military. During that time I had almost no contact with the veterans I served with in Charlie Company, with a couple of exceptions: Geoffrey Kerber survived and returned from Vietnam as a Buck Sergeant with two Bronze Stars for heroism in mid-1969, and we became lifelong friends. Bill Sommers calls from Wisconsin a couple times a year to commiserate and bitch with me about what went on over there and we have met for a couple of visits in Arizona.

In 1996 I managed to track down Sergeant Ed Ryan, who was by then Dr. Edward Ryan, working in psychology assisting veterans as well as non-veteran clients in Riverside, California. The occasion brought together a reunion of sorts for one night in Las Vegas with Ryan, Ed Crane, who was living in Oklahoma City, David Carter of Milwaukee, John Cleary from Cleveland and me. Some of the others were contacted but declined to attend, having long left Vietnam behind.

We sadly learned that Ron Cavett never fully recovered from the virulent strain of hepatitis he contracted in Vietnam. In poor and declining health he passed away as a result of the disease around 1980 while still a young man. Wayne Pope survived his tour and returned home to Georgia where he battled Post Traumatic Stress Disorder (PTSD), like so many of the rest of us who survived infantry duty with the Ninth Infantry Division in Vietnam.

Following his tour Bill Sommers quietly returned to family farming near Portage, Wisconsin where he kept his two Purple Hearts stashed away out of sight in the back of a drawer.

As for the role of the Ninth Infantry Division in Vietnam, it is worth noting the number of distinguished Generals who served as junior officers in the division over a three and one-half years of deployment there.

General Tommy Franks, wounded serving as a First Lieutenant in the artillery as a forward observer in the Ninth's First Brigade at Tan An near Tan Tru subsequently led the US Army's 2003 invasion of Iraq. General Wesley Clark, also wounded serving as a lieutenant in the Ninth Division became the Supreme Commander of NATO. General Eric Shinseki, wounded serving as a junior officer with the Ninth Division as an artillery forward observer subsequently became the Secretary of the Veterans

Administration following his retirement from the army' and the famous highly decorated Colonel David Hackworth commanded the 4th of the 39th Infantry Battalion of the Ninth in 1969.

For too many years following their service a great many veterans of Vietnam internalized their feelings, frustrations and emotions about the war they never asked for, many of them wincing silently as pundits and journalists spoke in glowing terms of the "Greatest Generation" while Baby Boomers carried the mantle of the "Me Generation"; while largely ignoring the legions of men and women of that generation who sacrificed and served bravely, and with great distinction a nation that for too many years largely ignored and even scorned their service.

Sacramento, California

2017

Contact the author at lfrankbrooks@gmail.com

Printed in Great Britain
by Amazon